Too Safe For Their Own Good?

Helping children learn about risk
and lifeskills

Jennie Lindon

NCB's vision is a society in which children and young people are valued, their rights respected and their responsibilities enhanced.

By advancing the well-being of all children and young people across every aspect of their lives, NCB aims to:
- reduce inequalities in childhood
- ensure children and young people have a strong voice in all matters that affect their lives
- promote positive images of children and young people
- enhance the health and well-being of all children and young people
- encourage positive and supportive family, and other environments.

NCB has adopted and works within the UN Convention on the Rights of the Child.

Published by NCB

NCB, 8 Wakley Street, London EC1V 7QE
Tel: 0207 843 6000
Website: www.ncb.org.uk
Registered charity number: 258825

NCB works in partnership with Children in Scotland (www.childreninscotland.org.uk) and Children in Wales (www.childreninwales.org.uk).

Second edition
First edition published 1999 by the National Early Years Network

ISBN: 978 1 907969 14 0

British Library Cataloguing in Publication Data
A catalogue record for this book is available from the British Library

Typeset by Saxon Graphics Ltd, Derby
Printed and bound by Hobbs the Printers Ltd, Totton, Hants SO40 3WX

Contents

In memory of Paul Bonel

Acknowledgements

A wide range of fellow professionals have been generous with their time and sharing their reflective practice. The thanks I expressed in the first edition of the book (1999) are still due to Annie Davy, the staff of Windale First School and of Grandpont Nursery and Ian Harris (all based in Oxfordshire at that time). Thank you to David Perkins (Kidsactive), Nikki Robinson (The Henley College) and Ruth Thomson (*Nursery World* magazine). My thanks also to the team from the Forest School and Children's Centre at Bridgwater College.

For this fully revised edition I want to add my thanks to Robin Duckett and Emma Pace (Sightlines Initiative) and to Claire Warden (Mindstretchers). I benefited from joining the woodland visits (part of Sightlines projects) with the nursery from Stocksfield Avenue Primary School (Newcastle-on-Tyne) and the reception class of Skerne Park Primary (Darlington). Thank you also to the team of The Rainbow Centre (Marham) and Dee Gent, manager, for bringing me up to date since my consultancy visit.

I am appreciative of the frank opinions expressed to me over the years by children and young people, a wide range of practitioners and also parents. I have changed the names of any children in the examples.

1 A Responsible Approach Towards Risk

In UK society 'official' childhood has become ever longer. In some ways the world of children has become more separate from that of adults. A distinction is sometimes appropriate, but it is not helpful to disrupt a positive pattern of integrating children slowly into adult responsibilities and pursuits. Even young children are keen to take on the role of 'apprentice' and to learn practical skills alongside familiar adults. Certainly it is, as they would say, 'so unfair!' when adolescents are over-protected in some ways, yet on other occasions told sharply to act their age. It is very hard to become more responsible over the years of adolescence, if familiar adults have failed to offer much in terms of practical lifeskills over the many years of childhood.

Practitioners and parents share the responsibility to teach children step by step how to keep themselves safe. Children's learning is a process lasting throughout the years of childhood and valuable experiences start in the very early years. Everyone needs to remember the main goal: that children are enabled to move towards being competent and confident adults. The current older generation needs to do a good job of sharing their grown-up skills and the fruits of their experience. Then this current generation of children will have a positive model to use with the next one.

Actual threats to children's safety

Practitioners and parents need to give well-informed safety messages to children. However, adults themselves can easily be misled over the real levels of everyday risk, because of the emphasis within the media. Newspapers, radio and television programmes make daily decisions about what is worthy of news coverage and which topics to develop into documentary programmes.

It is not unusual for parents, and children themselves, to express fear about the prospect of being seized, hurt and even killed by a total stranger (Tovey, 2007; Hawkins, 2010). This prospect of danger is often rated above injury or death on the road. Yet, the priority is the wrong way round: children are considerably more at risk from injury or death arising from a traffic accident than from attack by unknown adults. Children are more likely to be injured in accidents within their own home. Again in terms of reliable statistics (such as NSPCC, 2007) the far greater danger of deliberately inflicted harm on children comes from adults they already know, most often within their own family.

In the UK an extremely low number of children are abducted or killed by total strangers. The death or disappearance of any child or young person is one too many, but these heart-breaking incidents must be seen in context, and they are very rare. Serious injury or death from traffic accidents is unfortunately still common enough for these incidents not to attract national headlines. In contrast, the abduction or murder of a child by a stranger brings saturation media coverage. Adults, let alone children, become convinced that abduction and harm by strangers is commonplace, because they keep hearing about it and seeing the same small number of images recycled on different media.

The media also swings between two extremes. On the one hand are the lurid headlines that frighten many families into being highly protective, believing that society is now considerably more dangerous. Then, in quieter times for news, there is a tendency in the media to blame parents for 'wrapping children in cotton wool' and 'creating a generation of couch potatoes' through being deeply uneasy about letting their children out to play.

Very anxious adults

Any adult involved with children should, of course, be concerned for their safety and well-being. Registration and inspection services across the UK require that practitioners should have a high regard for safeguarding in the broadest sense (Lindon, 2008). However, a safe enough environment should not distort daily life for young children by removing a wide range of interesting experiences and resources.

An increasing preoccupation with even very low level risk can create a situation in which practitioners, or parents, continue to speculate on what might go wrong with a given experience. It is then very easy to lose sight of the potential benefits to children, for example, of being taken out and about in the local neighbourhood, climbing and clambering, or learning to be safe around sources of heat. The focus becomes that of keeping children away from an experience or resource that at some time they will encounter. Letters to early years magazines and the strands of conversation in chatrooms highlight the anxiety felt by many practitioners in taking responsibility for other people's children.

Without clear guidance on looking at the big picture, it can be tempting to embrace what has been described as 'the precautionary principle'. The atmosphere becomes what Tim Gill (2007) describes as 'risk averse': better not to take the chance, and be blamed for a near-miss or actual accident. Yet, children's learning will be undermined if valuable experiences, equipment and play materials are removed after one minor incident or because an adult voices concern about what 'might happen'.

The precautionary approach often assumes, wrongly, that it is possible to achieve a situation in which there are no accidents ever. But no environment will ever be 100 per cent safe. Even well-supervised children manage to hurt themselves, sometimes in unpredictable ways. As David Ball (2002) points out, a fair proportion of accidents, often minor, in school playgrounds are from trips and collisions in the context of ordinary play. Adults are responsible for avoiding preventable accidents, but a goal of zero risk is unrealistic. In fact, the precautionary approach itself entails a different kind of risk, that of an oppressive atmosphere for children and removal of significant benefits that they would have gained from appropriate play experiences.

Another issue is that practitioners, or parents, who analyse every situation in terms of what could go wrong, risk creating anxiety in some children and recklessness in others. Children learn a great deal about attitudes from familiar adults, but their personal approach also depends on their underlying temperament. Children who are inclined towards anxiety and a fearful outlook will be less able to address uncertain situations. Their peers who are by temperament more tolerant of uncertainty may have few ideas on how to handle risks they will encounter. Children do not benefit from having their play environment and daily experiences over-organised by adults who want to 'play it safe'. In fact the first casualties are a sense of playfulness and the power of learning through first hand experiences.

Building confidence, not anxiety

Since the 1990s, strong outdoor movements have developed across the UK, both in rural and urban areas. Over-anxiety about managing risk is not exclusive to outdoor activities, but adult caution has often focused on what could go wrong – rather than right – when young children enjoy generous amounts of time outdoors.

The Forest School movement started in Bridgwater, Somerset, in the 1990s, after a group of students from the college visited outdoors provision in Denmark. A team linked with the Children's Centre found and developed their own woodland site and established a model that has been followed in many other places. The overall aim is to introduce children as young as three and four to the natural world, beyond a garden, and to offer a setting in which they can learn about the outdoors, flora and fauna, the safe use of tools and natural materials, including about making fires (O'Brien and Murray, 2006).

The approach of the Sightlines Initiative (Duckett and Drummond, 2010) also focuses on the power of learning outdoors. This emphasis on working with children's interests has developed from the Reggio model (from northern Italy), with adults as enablers. Joint projects with schools bring young children into an area of woodland local to the school on a regular basis. Children are supported in learning about safety specific to the outdoors but with the scope for them to assess and manage their own level of risk.

All the outdoor projects place a high value on communication with families: explaining the importance of getting children out into the natural world and how children are kept safe without over-protection. Young children, and older, are able to explore at their own pace and there is significant effort in connecting the woodland outdoors experience with what happens back at nursery or reception class. Even the less sure among the children gain in confidence in an atmosphere of trust: children feel they can depend upon the adults, who in their turn demonstrate confidence in children's choices and good, supported judgement.

A change in the atmosphere?

It seems to be steadily less acceptable for any professional to announce, 'It's health and safety' or 'That's child protection' and expect to halt any discussion about questionable practices. Responsible professionals involved with children should be able to make a coherent case that this prohibition or that limit on experiences genuinely does make children safer and is really in their best interests (Lindon, 2008). Some kind of official stance and active support is needed. Otherwise children's experiences depend entirely upon the confidence of practitioners who take responsibility for their day.

The Health and Safety Executive (www.hse.gov.uk/risk) have taken an increasingly public line on sensible risk management. Pages on their website stress that it has never been the intention or recommendation of the HSE that safety should become overwhelmed with paperwork, or that it is possible to have no accidents whatsoever. HSE representatives have also become forthright in challenging claims that they are the people requiring children to wear goggles when playing conkers, stop pinning the tail on the donkey, or other persistent myths. In some instances these are the actions of a single setting converted into the utterly inaccurate claim of 'nobody's allowed anymore to…' by repeated media coverage.

Practitioners themselves should be willing to check and challenge newsworthy, but not necessarily accurate, stories about healthy and safety 'rules' – whether they are in the national media or travelling the local grapevine. It is professional to ask, 'who says this?' or 'where exactly did this happen?' It is unprofessional to add to the misinformation with an unquestioning passing on of, 'So now we've got to…' Do look at the HSE's *Myth of the Month* section www.hse.gov.uk/myth/

It is significant that Lord Young's report *Common Sense – Common Safety* to the government in October 2010 has recognised that it is inappropriate to treat low hazard environments such as schools and other places for children as if they are much the same as a factory. Recommendations include reversing the 'more is better' excesses in risk assessment paperwork, which some settings have felt obliged to follow. The proposals are for simpler forms of risk assessment for on-site activities in schools and similar settings and for taking children off-site for trips and outings. The advice is also to move from an exclusive risk assessment approach to a more rounded risk-benefit analysis, confirming the direction that thoughtful leaders and teams have already taken.

Risks and benefits

Responsible adults need to avoid knee-jerk reactions to visible hazards or the potential risk that they may present.

First of all, there is a difference between a **hazard** and a **risk**.

- A hazard is a physical situation that could potentially be harmful to children, or to anyone.
- A risk is the probability that the potential harm from this hazard will occur.

Risks are not absolutes; there are variations in the level of risk from different hazards. Risk assessment matters but a sensible process involves consideration of the genuine level of risk, the likely consequences if something does go wrong and the seriousness of those consequences should they occur.

Risk assessment in provision for children will frequently be best characterised by asking, 'what could I/we do?' Reflection and discussion is needed around the realistic steps that could be taken to minimise this risk so that children can continue to enjoy the experience, resource or equipment. It is not responsible adult behaviour to view risk assessment as thinking of the worst that could happen, assuming that adults are incapable of making any difference to the situation, and then banning, cancelling and removing in the name of safety.

The next crucial point to consider is that anxiety-driven risk assessment is often incomplete, because it overlooks potential **benefits**. The focus is all about what could go wrong through accidents or incidents, not about what children will lose if the particular experience or equipment is taken away from them. Early years, school and different types of out-of-school provision are not building sites or power stations. Risk assessment in settings for children should most usually be about getting to a 'yes' rather than a 'no', and to 'so long as...' rather than 'under no circumstances'.

The shift from risk assessment towards risk-benefit assessment (or analysis) has been a positive shift towards considering the big picture. It could well be described as doing a more thorough job of worrying. Practitioners need to consider the likely consequences of something going wrong because the environment is not completely child-safe. But what about the likely consequences for children, if a valuable experience is no longer available, a much-liked resource is taken away or a game that children cherish is banned by the grown-ups? Are there likely to be unforeseen negative consequences as a direct result of actions taken by adults worried about what has happened or might happen?

If there is a high risk of potential harm, and no benefit to children, then steps need to be taken to remove the hazard. A safe approach to domestic cleaning products like bleach in settings with young children is to keep them in locked cupboards. There are no positive consequences for young children in coming into contact with hazardous substances of this nature. On the other hand, scissors that will cut properly and craft glue that works need to be available within a learning environment where children are shown how to use these items appropriately. If children cannot learn to use effective tools, they will be unable to explore and create. It will not be appropriate for practitioners to do all the cutting and gluing in the name of health and safety.

Along with risk-benefit analysis another valuable concept has come to the forefront in recent years: taking a **proportionate** response to any given situation. For instance, water poses a hazard to young children because they can drown, even in shallow water. The danger arises partly because they cannot swim. Very young children do not close their mouths, instead they try to breathe or cry out, with tragic results. However, a responsible and proportionate approach cannot be to remove a valuable resource like water. Sources of water such as ponds or paddling pools can be made safe, partly by physical safety measures but largely by the behaviour of adults. Attentive grown-ups are the most important item of safety equipment in the whole situation. Young children can enjoy the delights of a paddling pool, or looking at the contents of a pond, when it is fully understood that an adult needs to remain by their side at all times.

The last useful concept to consider is that of **acceptable and unacceptable** risks. 'Risk' is not in itself negative and adults who become 'risk averse' (Gill, 2007) start to talk and behave as if it is beneficial to remove all sense of adventure from children's daily life. Ordinary life is full of risk taking: trying something out when there is no certainty. Young children need to feel confident of taking minor risks, intellectually and emotionally as well as physically, or else they will never stretch themselves in a positive way. Claire Warden and the Mindstretchers team (2010) stress the importance of being 'risk aware' instead of 'risk averse'. Adults need to make considered judgements about what the child wants to undertake, which include allowing a child to make that jump or clamber that which is within their abilities.

Nurseries and schools want to be welcoming, but they have to balance that with concerns for the security of the children. It is unacceptable if children can leave a setting without anybody realising, or if there is no clear line of responsibility for named children when groups go out on local trips. However, young children should be safe within the physical boundaries of any early years setting to the point where children – not babies – can explore indoors and in the garden without adults feeling they must be able to see all the children at all times. It would be a misunderstanding of acceptable and unacceptable risk if practitioners felt they could have no dens or other 'secret' places, because of the fear of what could be happening if children were not completely visible at all times.

Sometimes practitioners have specific, supported concerns about the behaviour of individual children, perhaps that a particular child's understanding of how to make friendly contact has been distorted through an abusive experience (Lindon, 2008). This situation has to be resolved by the key person, paying close attention to the child and how she or he approaches peers in cosy corners or places. It would be a disproportionate response to remove all such spaces on the basis that this child may behave inappropriately.

In terms of decisions made or ground rules developed, children have the right to expect consistency from the adults in the same setting. Young girls and boys should never find themselves caught in the middle between some practitioners who feel able to trust the children in given situations and practitioners within the same nursery, school or club whose default reaction is to say, 'No'. The unfortunate likely result is that children are pushed into different patterns of behaviour depending upon who is in charge at that moment. Alternatively, they may happily exploit the uncertainty generated by the inconsistent message from the adults by pushing the boundaries with, for example, 'But Jake lets us do it!' Or else children may simply become exasperated with adults in general and cease to listen or take much notice at all.

Another way of looking at hazard and risk

In the Rainbow Centre (Marham) there is a reminder notice for practitioners – although it is a positive message for any visiting adult, including parents. The notice says:

- A hazard is something a child does not see
- A risk is a challenge a child can see and chooses to undertake or not
- Eliminating risk leads to a child's inability to assess danger

The centre's approach to risk assessment includes discussion among adults about hazards: issues that adults know or anticipate could be problems but which under-fives are unlikely to recognise. The team's aim is to deal with those hazards that fall outside a child's knowledge and understanding. But the assessment is definitely that of securing benefits for children as well as reducing potential harm.

Different approaches are taken to dealing with hazards: sometimes they establish ground rules for an activity or occasionally designate a resource as one that always has an involved adult. But most often the approach is to offer assistance to children so they can practise and reach a level of competence where they no longer need adult support for this skill.

Another strand to the overall approach was to guide children, without nagging, to be aware of others around them. I was able to observe the effectiveness of this underlying guidance. Many of the three- and four-year-olds moved at speed around the garden by running, on bikes or by clambering up and down the little hill. Yet they showed considerable attention to avoiding bumps or crashes with other children.

Rainbow practitioners were ready to make comments in ways that gave children scope to change their behaviour. For instance, one child was digging energetically in the sand, with the result that some sand was being flung around. The practitioner involved in this activity said calmly, 'When you're doing that, you're putting sand on everyone else.' Her suggestion was that the unwanted sand needed to go to the side. The child came up with the idea of using a bucket, which was greeted with, 'Good idea!'

2 Learning about Safety up to Middle Childhood

Children learn about safety over the many years of childhood and then of adolescence. A firm grasp of how to keep themselves safe grows with their understanding of the world, general knowledge, and direct first hand experiences, which in turn support learning. It is tempting to want certainties, such as, 'How old should children be before they are left alone at home?' But like so much of child development, there are no absolute ages by which children can be expected to understand given issues of safety. There are only general guidelines for what they are likely to be able to understand. So a more sensible and useful question is always, 'What do children need to have learned *before* they are left on their own, or *before* they can be trusted to keep themselves safe in any given situation?'

Whether in the family home, in early years, school or out-of-school settings, there is always room for informed judgement when deciding whether or not a child is able to deal with a particular risk. Thoughtful adults weigh up not only the age and ability of individual children, but also their familiarity with the particular young boy or girl, their temperament and how they tend to behave. Children learn within a social and cultural context, and this point is as true for learning safety and competence as with any other aspect of their development. Children's potential for learning is shaped by adults' attitudes towards taking an active role in helping children become more independent and the things that are judged to be the priorities in daily life.

Some families place a high value on helping children learn skills that give them a clear role and responsibilities within family life. Generalisations are problematic, but in UK society as a whole, a tendency has evolved of complaining that children fail to learn how to take care of themselves or help out at home. Yet, at the same time, an unchallenged agreement has emerged that everyone is so short of time 'nowadays' that families cannot share household tasks with children in an age-appropriate way. It is hard to assess the extent, but anecdotal evidence suggests that a proportion of parents are tempted to do everything themselves 'because it is quicker' rather than showing children how to be competent in those tasks.

The following highlights of how children grow and learn about safety provide guidance for appropriate adult responses and suggestions about experiences for children at different points in their development.

Under ones

Babies have no understanding of safety and risk. They have neither the words nor the general experience to make any sense of adult warnings. Their strong motivation to use their growing physical skills, and an otherwise valuable curiosity, will get them into danger unless they are closely and affectionately supervised with an alert eye and ear.

Safety equipment, such as stair gates, contributes to a safe environment, as does careful attention to ensure that play materials are suitable for babies. Resources for babies and very young children need to stand up to rough treatment, have no small removable parts and be safe to go in the mouth. But these measures are not enough on their own. Unless babies are safely asleep or resting in their cot, responsible adults should be able to see and hear them easily. Purchased safety equipment will not do the job without an attentive adult.

Even in an appropriately safe learning environment, babies and very young children will show interest in items that are not safe for them to hold or mouth. Early years group settings are unlikely to have items within a baby's reach indoors that are unsuitable for play. However, babies need to get outdoors just as much as young children and a safe enough garden will have items that should not go into a baby's mouth. Childminders or nannies in a family home may need to encourage babies or very young children away from the real telephone with a decommissioned one of their own, or a suitable toy phone.

Sometimes babies need to be gently held and little hands removed from something – usually more than once. Any 'no' or 'no touching' should be said gently and an alternative offered that is safe. Sometimes it is appropriate to say, and show, 'We look at the rabbit. We don't poke him.'

In the end it is counterproductive to try to remove everything that a baby or toddler should not mouth. A supportive adult models the interest of exploration by looking and listening, and shows gentle touching. It is important to think about how to satisfy babies' curiosity rather than keep taking items away. Interesting play resources are not always bought toys but include items that are safe for babies to hold, wave around and mouth (Lindon, 2006).

Toddlers and young twos

During the second year of life, very young children gain a great deal of experience in familiar settings. They build up the physical understanding of what they can do and some grasp of what leads to tumbles, but there are limits to their ability to connect cause and effect in daily life. Individual experiences of falls or bumps are not necessarily translated into an understanding that something is unsafe. It is very important that adults do not get cross with young children who appear to put themselves at risk or 'don't listen to a word I say!'

One reason for toddlers' apparent lack of learning is that they can be so absorbed in what they want to do that they, for example, forget the set of steps as they run. Coupled with this is the limited knowledge of cause and effect: they do not realise that the same bump may result if they undertake the same action. So toddlers often do not understand why and how they got hurt until adults explain to them patiently and more than once. They do not yet grasp the concept that they 'might' hurt themselves, or the logic of 'if' they do something 'then' they will get hurt. Very young children often need to be guided and helpful adults have to show and tell them how to stay safe.

Toddlers and young twos are ready to begin an understanding that some domestic household items are not for them to touch. It is wise to start the process and help them learn how to distinguish between objects that are:

- entirely for their use
- to be used by them only with adult help
- definitely only for adults to use.

For instance, in a nursery or family home it may be that the big scissors are only for grown-ups to use, whereas the small scissors are for use by children. These scissors still have to be efficient for cutting or else they are useless as a tool for children. For things that are out of bounds, an explanation and demonstration by adults will help toddlers understand that 'this is too high/too sharp/too hot for you'. Wise adults offer an alternative such as, 'but you can watch me', 'you can hold this for me' or 'you can have this instead'.

Three to five years of age

Between three and five years, children can build significant knowledge of their familiar world, so long as they are enabled to enjoy a wide range of first hand experiences (Rich and others, 2005). Their physical skills have developed. So young girls and boys are increasingly able to undertake ordinary tasks that require good hand–eye coordination and careful attention to what they are doing. Within this age range, children will be ready to be trusted with some activities that were not possible when they were younger. Adults therefore need to monitor themselves on a regular basis. Watch out for an unreflective habit of saying to a child: 'You're too little' – maybe they can help, or could if the task were made a little simpler. Adults cannot keep on saying, 'You can do that when you're older'; when is 'older' going to arrive?

An atmosphere in which children can learn independence

The focus at the Rainbow Centre (Marham) is to encourage all children to build the confidence to be independent learners. Practitioners are easily available because the team take the appropriate perspective that, for young children, being independent is definitely not the same as being left without help.

Practitioners were ready to offer advice or assistance about technique, but equally they also watched and admired. One example was by a clambering area with a slide, walkway and potential jump-off point. Children of both sexes used this equipment throughout the day. But I especially watched four boys (all older threes or fours) who spent a sustained period of time practising various ways to jump or semi-jump from this equipment.

Two boys chose to jump from the platform, another to go down the pole and the fourth developed a slide off the platform from a sitting position. The children were able to decide upon and practise their techniques because they knew the adults were supportive of more adventurous physical activity. Twice the same practitioner came close and watched in an encouraging way, clapping and giving the thumbs-up for the different kinds of jumps. The boys all landed securely with only one exception: a child went slightly off balance on landing. But he rubbed his hand, brushed himself off and went straight back up again.

The practitioners at Rainbow are also alert to less sure children who are swift to say, 'I can't'. The aim is to encourage children away from a helpless outlook whilst respecting their concerns. The consistent team approach is to enable children to manage small risks, to stretch them a little within an experience that they are currently uncertain they can manage.

It is possible to observe the impact of experiences on young boys and girls, including adult attitudes that allow boys more risk than their female peers. Again, it is problematic to generalise across families, but quite a few parents still seem ready to direct their daughters to 'be careful' yet allow, even expect, their sons to be physically more outgoing and take risks. There is, of course, a great deal of variety within children of each sex as well as their parents. But all children will be influenced by the breadth of experiences available.

Early years teams that value outdoor play and encourage adventurous activities find that many girls rise happily to the challenge, just as much as boys (Lindon, 2010). Of course, some young girls are cautious: 'I might hurt myself', or have accepted the message that the more lively activities are only for boys. All children deserve to be encouraged to stretch themselves a little beyond their current comfort zone. Boys deserve consideration just as much as girls. Boys with a more cautious temperament can be put under undue pressures by adults who believe 'real boys' throw themselves into rumbustious activity. Boys, just as much as girls, have the right to step by step support to ease them beyond their current level of comfort.

The language of these young children has developed further, in terms of their own speech and how far they understand what adults say and explain. Children are also more able to think ahead, to remember what they were told on a previous occasion and to consider that something 'might' happen. They are more able to make connections between experiences, so long as adult explanations or warnings are combined with active demonstration, telling and showing.

Children's social and emotional development is also highly relevant here. Young children gain immense satisfaction in learning how to do something new. Perhaps they are now 'big enough' to be shown how to carry the jar of strawberry jam safely from room to room. Children not only gain from new physical skills, their sense of self-worth is boosted when they feel trusted to do something by an adult. Children become more confident through experiences that help them to feel competent in their own social world.

However, adults must not over-estimate young threes' abilities or even the level of knowledge of five-year-olds who still have a very great deal to learn about their world. Under-fives, even under-eights, are sometimes very literal: a safety message about looking out for cars may not be generalised to bicycles. Or adult warnings about care around heat in the kitchen may have overlooked that a pan or hotplate can still be very hot, even though the gas is turned off or the red glow has disappeared. Even children in middle childhood do not always understand what an adult has explained. They sometimes forget the safety message and sometimes they just do not want to follow it, because the consequence seems to be loss of playful enjoyment. Recall that adults sometimes act in ways they know are unsafe such as dashing across the road without looking to catch the bus.

Five to eight years of age

Children in this age group can be very competent in practical lifeskills as long as they have been given opportunities to learn and practise. First hand experience is crucial, and neither skills nor knowledge simply appear with the passing of another birthday. Telling children is not enough; they need to have plenty of experience of undertaking tasks, initially with a supportive adult. If they have been enabled to learn relevant ideas and skills, children in this age range can have a broad understanding of risks and be able to take some sensible safety measures for themselves.

However, there is still much to learn and some gaps in the understanding of children who are still relatively young. Children may genuinely not understand the limits to their skills. For instance, they can run fast, but not fast enough to cross the road before the speeding car. They can swim, but a fast flowing river is a very different proposition from a swimming pool. Children all want some challenge and settings that are too safety-conscious can be boring. If given a choice, children may simply decide not to attend this kind of setting. Otherwise they will tend to take one of two equally negative options, to:

■ sit about being bored by passive activities and learning very little
■ or create some level of danger in the setting through their use of the play equipment, their created games or behaviour with each other.

The pattern of development is not only influenced by a child's age and their experiences but also by individual temperament. Some children are by nature more adventurous than others, and such individual differences will have been further shaped by their life experience to date. As much as children have learned, there will still be gaps in their knowledge which adults may not notice unless they take the time to listen to children. To give children this attention may be especially hard when adult and child have just had a disagreement about safety issues. Conversations with a child are just as important as clear safety rules. Sometimes this personal communication is more important and, certainly, no set of safety rules, however wise, will do the job without adult observation, listening and talking with familiar children.

Children with disabilities or chronic illness

Disabled children need to share much of the same experience as other children of the same age range. It is important that practitioners and parents do not over-react to a child's disability or continuing health condition. It is understandable that adults can be concerned and keen to protect a disabled or very sick child. However, disabled children have the same motivation to learn and grow in competence as their peers. The adult response should be proportionate to the extra care and attention that this child actually needs in comparison with peers.

The learning environment in nursery, school, out-of-school provision or a family home needs to be as safe as is appropriate for disabled children, allowing for specific issues around mobility and level of understanding. There may be some issues of protection from risks which are specific to a child's chronic health condition. However, these issues need to be assessed on an individual basis and, as far as possible, discussed with the children themselves. Adults need to develop good habits of talking with children about any safety issues.

■ Can children and their parents or other family carer gain easy access to the setting or play provision in the first place?
■ Disabled children share some issues around easy access with their age peers. Can all the children reach play materials, food or books without having to stretch or clamber in an unsafe way?
■ Is the learning environment organised to create opportunities for any child to make choices between experiences and activities?
■ Are the working surfaces at the right level and is there space for a child to move easily in a wheelchair or with a walking frame?

- Disabled children should be enabled to move about and use materials and facilities, with the understanding that they will have some falls and spills, like any child.

Children with learning disabilities may need adult awareness that what is developmentally appropriate for that child may not be age related. Depending on the kind and severity of a learning disability, children may need much simpler practice, finer steps of experience in order to learn, and longer periods of time at the different stages of learning than their peers. Perhaps there will always be a ceiling on their understanding and competence, but this must not be allowed to remain lower than necessary. Disabled children need and deserve the same 'you can do it' approach, supported by the advice and encouragement that should be offered to any child.

3 Dealing with Incidents and Accidents

However well-supervised the setting, there will inevitably be some accidents and near-misses. Children can learn from what has happened when familiar adults reflect on what has happened, rather than over-react.

Concern over what might happen

It is an unwise habit for adults to express safety concerns as absolute fact, such as 'Come down off that wall. You'll fall and hurt yourself.' Unless this is a very high wall, the more likely situation is that the adult is concerned about possible risk: that children may not be safe balancers or they may get distracted and fall. More confident children, or those whose enjoyment overcomes any concerns, will keep climbing and wall walking, although they may ensure it is at a time when they cannot be observed. If children do not fall, then the adult becomes less credible to them and probably more tedious. More wary children may take the message to heart, stop doing an activity they had enjoyed and perhaps lose a chance to grow in physical confidence and skills. Wall walking is enjoyable and low wall walking is safe, because the adult can offer a hand.

It is important to avoid shouting at children. The only justification for calling out a loud warning is when the adult is at a distance and the child is genuinely in a risky situation. Even then, panic-stricken shouting by adults may distract a child's attention and put them in more danger of falling or over-balancing. Concerned adults have to make that split-second decision.

- Use calm words, with useful verbal prompts such as, 'Watch carefully where you put your feet' or 'Please sit and finish your sandwich, then you can run about'.
- Offer a hand to a child balancing on a low wall or on an obstacle course and let them decide if they need this support. When a less sure child decides to go it alone, they deserve a, 'Well done! You don't need my helping hand any more.'
- Consider being honest with a child when it is you who is uneasy. It might be as simple as, 'Just for my sake, please check where you're going to land before you're in mid-air.'
- Considerate adults are willing to reflect on their own swift reactions. Bad habits can develop of saying, 'No, you can't do that!' or 'Stop it right now!' before even considering the genuine level of danger.

Teams and individuals who value physical activity for children, often linked with generous time outdoors, aim to make a situation safe so that children can continue with their activity. Discussion within a team is important, so that children never experience a situation in which one person says, 'Go for it!' and their colleague says, 'Come down this instant!' Children should not be left to negotiate the gap created by inconsistency between adults in the same place, whether in the family home or outside.

In woodland with the Skerne Park reception class

This group of four- and five-year-olds go once a week with their practitioners to visit an area of woodland in a joint project with Sightlines Initiative. The children travel with their reception practitioners and then walk through the woodland area to where the Sightlines team are waiting – having set up the base between the trees and hoisted the flag. One of the Sightlines team plays the violin once the children can be heard in the near distance. The children learn to follow the sound of the music as well as look out for the flag. The same person also plays the children out of the woodland when they leave at the end of the morning's visit.

In this morning session all the children were busy with their chosen pursuits. They knew to stay within sight of the flag, unless they went off adventuring with an adult. This excursion happened when two boys went with an adult to search for a patch where it would be possible to look up at the sun through the tree canopy.

Children challenge themselves physically and both sexes are adventurous in climbing and clambering. One tree is known as the climbing tree and is especially welcoming, with low branches. The agreement between the adults is that they do not lift children up into a tree.

Children climb where and however they are able by their own abilities and current size and strength. Adult support was in terms of possible strategies and treating a situation as a problem that might be solved with good ideas. Adults are ready to remind children to be aware when branches are wet from heavy rain and to test a new section before putting their full weight on a branch. The only ground rule is that children do not climb higher than an adult could reach them, in case they did get stuck.

The base camp is equipped with ropes and any possible strategy, or attempt at making something, is a joint enterprise between an adult and children, who are fully involved in the designing as well as in the actual making. During this morning, children were keen to create a hammock – which gradually sunk during the morning and became an equally interesting resource for individual children to wrap and 'hide' themselves in. Rope, secure knots and branches were also part of chosen strategies for clambering. Under these circumstances children talked with an adult about the problem they wanted to solve and how they might do it.

A set of parallel ropes had been secured between two trees before the children's arrival. Different children were busy on this resource for all of the morning. The challenge for them was how to get themselves onto the ropes at one end, as well as move along them, by hand holds on the upper rope and moving their feet along the lower rope. Individual children explored and established different strategies, which they then showed to other children, as well as to the adults.

When something nearly happens

When something nearly happens to a child, responsible adults often experience an unpleasant mix of strong emotions that can get in the way of a response that will be helpful to the child. It is not unusual that adults feel:

- fear for what could have happened, plus a sense of shock
- guilt for the moment of adult inattention
- frustration that earlier safety warnings have been so easily forgotten by the child or small group
- embarrassment because of the actual or possible reactions of onlookers, combined with a concern about being criticised and blamed.

Adults are understandably shaken when they see a child hurt or emerging from being temporarily lost in a large store or mall. However, what are children to make of times, relatively common occurrences in streets and parks, when the prominent adult emotion is anger? It is not unusual to observe an adult, who has just saved a child from walking onto the road, shouting at the child and/or even smacking her. In calmer moments parents tend to justify this reaction on the grounds that, 'He has to learn what's dangerous.'

It is possible to have fellow feeling for the fraught adults. Yet children are utterly bemused and, often, distressed – sometimes more by the adult reaction than by the averted danger, which they did not even realise was there. Children cannot learn anything useful about safety and keeping themselves safe when messages are lost in adult anger. Children may conclude that they are 'naughty' or 'stupid', and certainly that they have made their parent or other carer very cross. But young children are left confused about what exactly they have done wrong and certainly about what to do to be right next time. The adult's anger blurs the safety message and provokes emotions in the children that can actually block useful learning.

Children can only learn from a near-miss if adults manage to regulate their own feelings.

- It can be tough in the heat of the moment, but practitioners and parents need to remain as calm as possible and not load their own fears and shock onto the child.
- Do your utmost to avoid cross words, blame or unhelpful cries such as, 'I told you not to …!' or 'How many times have I said…?'
- Treat the incident as an error on the part of the child: a poor choice, perhaps a very unwise decision but not as intentional 'bad behaviour'.
- Children cannot learn from their mistakes, if the experience is overwhelmed by negative feelings: distress because the adult is shouting or embarrassment at being roundly criticised in front of other people.
- Maybe there is good reason to judge that older children have knowingly put themselves in danger. Then there needs to be a serious conversation about the unwise choice they made.
- If adults remain calm, there is more chance that useful information will emerge. For example, perhaps this child, or small group, felt under serious pressure from other children and could not work out how to extricate themselves from the given situation.
- Adults need to be honest, wherever possible, explaining their reaction and feelings simply to the child, especially if they failed to avoid shouting. It may help to share with a child, 'I was scared for you' or 'I would be so upset if you were hurt', along with, 'I'm sorry. I shouldn't have yelled like that.'

- Sometimes the first priority is to comfort children who are upset, for instance because they realised they were lost or they belatedly recognise how close they came to being seriously injured.

It is wise to have a conversation about the incident. However, sometimes it is better to wait a little after the event, when everyone has calmed down. It would be unhelpful to delay this for too long, though. A short break within the same day may be handy before, say, the starter of, 'I'd like to talk to you about the swing', about the child who walked in front of a set of swings, oblivious to the fact that these were about to come back into the child's path. Be ready to listen to older children's explanations or comments, including perhaps their view that they were not doing anything dangerous at all. If adults disagree with a child, then they need to explain rather than simply assert, 'I know better'.

When something happens

However hard adults try, children will sometimes get hurt in an early years, school or out-of-school setting. In a safe enough learning environment, most of the incidents will be minor. However, the way that practitioners handle events can offer greater, or fewer, positive lessons to children. The wise responses from adults have much in common with how they handle near-misses, as described above, but there can be additional issues when children have hurt themselves, have injured another child or when something else has gone wrong.

- Adults need to stay calm so the children feel confident someone has taken kindly control.
- Children need to experience a responsible adult model who moves in on the scene, checks out what has happened without adding to the panic or drama, and sets about helping any child who has been hurt.
- Other children may be genuinely concerned, but a large interested audience may not be helpful. A hurt child may well want peace and breathing space.
- However, let other children be a safe part of how the incident is handled. It may be necessary to send a trusted child to tell another adult what has happened.
- A close friend or sibling may want to sit beside or hold the hand of the child who is hurt. So long as the injured child is happy with the support, do not automatically direct other children away. Thank the friend or sibling afterwards for their help.

- It is best to say out loud to children what needs to be done in terms of basic first aid for cuts or bruises. Adults can explain in simple words that they need to clean the dirt out of a cut or that a cold compress will help a bang on the forehead.
- Be honest with them and do not say something will not hurt when it is likely to sting.
- Basic first aid treatment is part of the adult duty of care. Practitioners should know if individual children have allergies that affect what is appropriate and safe.
- Listen to how the children feel and attend to what they say hurts them. It is disrespectful to children when adults dismiss children's words or pained expression with remarks like: 'You're making a fuss about nothing' or 'That didn't hurt!'

All settings, including schools, should have a proper understanding of safeguarding which absolutely does **not** mean that children are denied touch, comfort or proper first aid in the name of child protection (Lindon, 2008). It is indeed a safeguarding issue, but the point is that refusal to care for a hurt or distressed child 'because we're not allowed to have any physical contact' could well be judged as neglect. The adult behaviour also borders on emotional abuse, because of the likely feelings of a child who is expected to attend to their own grazed knee. The same applies for children who are expected to deal with the physical consequences of their toileting accident, or sit in soiled clothes until a parent had been summoned. The deeply misguided notion that 'no-touch' policies should be part of safeguarding is now being challenged at a more consistent, official level. See, for instance, Michael Gove's open letter (6 January 2011) about an NSPCC training programme on child protection and music teachers www.education.gov.uk/inthenews/inthenews/a0072100/letter-from-michael-gove-on-music-teaching

Some incidents leading to injury will provoke a conversation between adults and children along the lines of: 'What happened here?' or 'What went wrong with…?' Avoid having this kind of conversation at the same time as dealing with hurt children. The presence of a newly injured child can make the whole situation fraught and it is too easy to jump to conclusions about what happened or even who is most at fault. Children may have mixed feelings about an event. Even the child who was hurt may be distressed if other children receive punishment that is disproportionate to what happened. Children can also be put in a very uncomfortable position if their accident leads to an absolute ban on an activity that everyone enjoyed.

For incidents that merit a later conversation:

- Talk calmly with any children who were involved. Wise adults show very clearly that they do not have preconceptions about who is likely to have been to blame.
- Invite comments and listen carefully, avoiding an atmosphere of cross-questioning. Children may view adult questions as an interrogation to assign blame. So it is crucial to talk and act in a way that is clearly not judgemental. Over time, children will believe that familiar adults are honest when they say: 'I want to know what happened.'
- Consider any sensible consequences as a result of what has been learned. Individual children may need to recognise the consequences of their actions on themselves or others, or perhaps a play area needs a more regular adult presence – friendly, but ensuring everyone is behaving in a safe way.

Practitioners should make time to talk with a child's parents, even for minor bumps and scrapes. The key person in a group setting should explain what happened and how the incident was handled. Any incident will have been written up into the accident book of the setting or by the childminder. Some provisions follow a policy of asking a parent to read and sign the entry or a single form used for this purpose. It is important to communicate the message that the incident is now closed. It is not fair if this child is reprimanded or even punished for being 'careless'. Nor is it appropriate for parents to tackle other children who were involved – often their names would not be mentioned in the description of the incident.

Alternatives to bans

A sensible adult response to an accident, or series of related incidents, must of course include reflection and discussion over whether any changes are needed in daily practice. However, there can be serious negative consequences when adults respond with an absolute ban on an enjoyable play activity. Anecdotal evidence continues to provide examples of some early years and school settings who still react to incidents or minor skirmishes by prohibiting play activities such as football, lively games of tag and some pretend games that children clearly enjoy. Such decisions are usually local, or even single setting rulings, and not what 'they' in the government require in the name of Health and Safety.

To unreflective adults, the advantages to a ban on an activity or specific play resources are that:

- children cannot be injured
- adults feel they have responded effectively and 'done something' about it.

However, there are disadvantages to outright bans.

- Children feel aggrieved, especially since bans are usually imposed without a proper discussion of alternatives. They are likely to feel that boring adults have stopped an activity important in their social world.
- The opportunity has been lost to take a problem-solving approach with children and for them to learn through being involved in this process.
- Even though parents voice serious concerns because their child has been hurt, many parents are increasingly unhappy about bans as a frontline approach to dealing with lively games or favourite play items for children.

It is striking that bans are usually only applied to activities or play resources that practitioners judge are of marginal importance or offer little or no 'educational value'. Bans are not usually imposed when safety issues are raised about activities or equipment that adults regard as a legitimate part of the nursery or school day. In that situation adults usually focus on the behaviour of an individual or group: that it is never acceptable to poke people with pencils or bang them on the head with a book.

A risk and benefit assessment helps a team to consider the situation more calmly and from every angle, not only from an adult perspective. An additional approach, especially when children's games or play possessions are involved, is to invite the children's involvement in a problem-solving way.

Gymnastics on the bridge

The Rainbow Centre (Marham) has developed exciting special areas in the garden. One of these is a bark covered Trim Trail, which includes a low suspended wooden bridge section. A lot of the children (over threes) loved wrapping their legs around the rails of the bridge on the trim trail, suspending themselves from the secure rails. Some of the more physically adventurous children – girls as well as boys – liked to turn themselves upside down, let go and land back on their feet. The manager asked me to observe this activity during my consultancy and give my considered opinion.

I agreed that this form of gymnastics bordered on being rather frightening to observe as an adult. I took a deep breath and could see the temptation of saying children should not do what I then called the upside-downs. It says a lot for the commitment of the Rainbow team that they had not yet stopped the children; the adults wanted an environment safe enough for children to take risks. I watched a whole series of children doing their upside-downs. They were physically adept and managed the manoeuvre many times without mishap. They enjoyed doing this challenging action. Also the less confident children were motivated to try it and very willing to ask for and accept help from the practitioner nearby.

I agreed with the manager's preference not to call a halt to this physical activity. But it also made sense to consider a few ground rules, to be agreed within the Rainbow team and communicated to the children. I made several suggestions and the manager later let me know that they adopted three practical rules, which were made into a notice with visuals that was then fixed to the bridge area.

The ground rules, which children have found to be reasonable, are that:

1. The upside-down sequence is always done with two 'strong' hands.
2. Children only do upside-downs when there is an adult by the bridge.
3. No more than two children do upside-downs at the same time.

There have been no accidents from this lively form of gymnastics in the two years since my consultancy with Rainbow. A final point, which I shared with the Rainbow team, is that enthusiastic practitioners need to be aware of their own physical well-being, for instance, in supporting manoeuvres. 'Watch your back' is an important adult safety reminder.

The problem-solving approach

Adults have a responsibility for children in their setting, but all adults also have an obligation to consider the consequences of their own actions. An alternative to bans is to take a problem-solving approach that involves the children, and possibly parents as well, in a discussion about ways in which a game could continue without near-misses or minor injuries.

The basic steps in effective problem-solving are to:

1. enable a full discussion about the nature of the problem
2. generate a range of possible answers to 'what could we do about this problem?'

3. decide on the best solution out of those discussed
4. put the proposed solution into action for long enough to see if and how it works
5. monitor and evaluate the situation, and discuss again as necessary.

Such discussions with children only work if adults give their time and attention. Children of any age are unimpressed with practitioners or parents who claim to want to hear the children's ideas, fail to listen and then push through their own favourite adult solution. Open discussion about a problem area in a nursery or school can be a productive way forward on a particular issue. This adult choice also gives children first hand experience of problem solving over issues that matter to them.

Step 1: Full discussion of the problem

A proper discussion allows everyone to voice their views without interruption, name-calling or other put-downs – from either the adults or the children. Adults can set the scene by establishing basic ground rules for listening, avoiding interruptions and commenting on other people's ideas without discourteous remarks. The adults have a major responsibility to model good listening behaviour, especially if there is no previous tradition of listening and problem-solving in the setting.

Within an open discussion, adults can take their turn to explain to children, or to child class representatives in a school council, how they – the adults – see the problem. It is important that adults voice their concerns with honest, descriptive comments such as: 'I'm worried about children being hit by conkers' rather than put-downs such as: 'You're all so careless.' Adults may also express general concerns about fairness, for instance, that the football game seems to take up a significant amount of space in the playground.

However, adults must also listen, without arguing or interrupting, to the children's perspective on the situation. It is the adults' responsibility to work to understand and show that they have grasped the children's perspectives. Make sure that all the perspectives on the problem are heard. Consider with the children whether issues, concerns and then possible ways forward need to be recorded and, if so, in what ways.

Perhaps a discussion starts because the adults feel the football game in the playground has become too rumbustious, not to mention the broken window.

- Perhaps the football players say that the playground offers them their only chance to play the game, and apologise about the window.
- Some children feel harassed by the energetic activity of the footballers and say that the game runs over other places and spaces to interrupt their play.
- However, some other boys or girls complain that the informal football team is a clique, not letting other children join the game. They want to play as well, not have the football stopped.

It is important to hold back from talking about possible solutions before the problem has been thoroughly discussed. Until children understand this aspect of effective problem solving, it is crucial that the adult facilitating the discussion acts as a guide. Even four- and five-year-olds are able to follow the flow of thorough exploration of 'what's happening' before the discussion moves on to 'what can we do about it?'

Step 2: Generate and discuss a range of possibilities

Encourage the children to contribute possible solutions to a problem.

- Ensure that all ideas for tackling the problem – whether generated by child or adult – are given a proper hearing.
- Take time to talk around ideas and help children to understand that there is no need to jump at the first or second idea.

Step 3: Choosing a solution from a range of possibilities

Look at the range of ideas in terms of how each might work and what would be important if this solution is to work.

- Children need to be sure there is equal consideration of their ideas as well as those put forward by the adults. This is a proper discussion, not a pretend one in which the grown-ups are going to insist on their solution.
- Practitioners can be honest about their responsibilities and any issues that are non-negotiable in the setting. Be clear with children also about where there is genuine room for manoeuvre.
- Reach agreement about which solution will be tried; ideally a full agreement but, if not, at least a good working majority vote. If a note

is kept of all the ideas, then children may feel their idea could be brought back.

- Agree on the specific responsibilities of both adults and children, if everyone is to give this solution its best chance.
- Set a realistic time deadline for giving the idea a proper run and agree on when to talk again. In an early years setting or the home of a childminder, this discussion may be relatively informal – at key group time or a conversation over tea.
- If appropriate, draft a letter to parents, with children's input, explaining the situation and what is being done. Direct communication will be welcome when parents have expressed concern about this problem. In some provision, this communication may go onto the website or be emailed to families.

Step 4: Idea into action

Practitioners in any setting must keep their part of the bargain and ensure that any colleagues do likewise. Children will brand adults as untrustworthy and promise-breakers if they back down on their word or abandon the agreed solution at the first minor difficulty. Some interim discussion and reminders may be useful to keep a potentially good idea on track.

Step 5: Monitoring and evaluation through discussion

It is important to monitor how the solution is working from the different perspectives of adults and children. Talk again informally with the children, or class representatives in school, to evaluate whether the problem is resolved. Is the activity now going ahead in a safer and fairer way for all concerned? If there are continuing problems, discuss possible solutions.

Emotional support following serious incidents

Even appropriately safe provision may experience a serious accident within the setting or an external incident such as being involved in a traffic collision during the regular mini-bus trips to the swimming pool. It is also possible that children will experience or witness a serious accident within their family time. It is very likely that their feelings and reactions will spill over into their time in nursery or school. If a child, or family member, is visibly injured, other children in nursery or club are almost bound to notice and raise the topic in conversation.

A research project by the Child Accident Prevention Trust (CAPT) has shown how much children need emotional support after accidents and how often this need fails to be met, especially if children's physical injuries are minor. (Details of leaflets about this project can be found in the Resources section on p. 78.) Children who have witnessed an accident in which a friend or sibling was injured can be very distressed. However, their emotions might be overlooked because they were not directly hurt themselves.

Adults are sometimes uncertain about how to handle the aftermath of such incidents. There can still be considerable resistance to giving children an opportunity to talk on the grounds that 'they will only get upset all over again, so it's better to leave it'. Adults who are confused about how to handle the situation may also decide that supportive conversation is best left to 'experts'. Unreflective practitioners or parents may also conveniently convince themselves that children do not feel experiences in the same way that adults do and that 'children soon forget'.

The underlying emotion and reasoning here might be one of finding an excuse not to talk with children, especially when the adults are distressed. Of course, adults themselves often need support under these circumstances – for themselves, but also so they can support children. Practitioners should be able to find support within their own team or network and they should, in turn, feel able to offer some support to parents, besides being able to direct parents to local resources for support. A request for a listening ear at any time should never be ignored.

Familiar adults are often the best people to help distressed children, who may not welcome being expected to talk with a stranger, however kindly. Expertise in this area is often best shared by an appropriate professional with the familiar adult who spends days with the child. Some key issues are to:

- Listen to the children and let them talk as and when they wish to.
- Respect children's feelings and understand that some effects of accidents or of being a witness to a distressing incident can last for weeks and months, not just days.

■ Let children judge whether it is more upsetting for them to talk or to remain silent. It is for the children themselves to judge whether they feel they have 'got over it'.

Attentive adults are guided by the children over what they find distressing and why. For instance, children may feel that an injury resulting from a game or sports activity is not a source of distress because 'these things happen'. On the other hand, a less serious physical injury sustained in a road accident may be far more upsetting to children, because of their complete lack of control over the circumstances. Practitioners or parents who are supporting a child often need someone with whom they can talk, for reassurance or guidance on whether additional help is now needed. Children sometimes play out their worries, as well as or instead of talking them through. Professionals involved with children need additional training to undertake play therapy as such, but a familiar adult, such as a child's key person, is in a strong position to help informally through play and conversation.

It is equally important to find out and listen to what children feel will help them, rather than assuming that adults know best. For instance, a child who has handled an accident with fortitude may not want public recognition in school assembly or a glossy certificate for bravery. Check with children how they feel before organising a public event that seems like a good idea to adults. When asked, 'we were thinking about…', 'how would you feel if …?', some children might be delighted but others may indicate that they do not want this event. Some children just want to be treated as what they regard as completely normally, apart from having easy access to time and attention from a caring adult who will listen when they want to talk.

Inevitably some early years, school or out-of-school provision will be touched by tragedy or an unexpected internal crisis. It is responsible to have written procedures for dealing with a critical incident (Rowling, 2003). However, this kind of written preparation is not to distance adults from emotions, which will have to be faced when the crisis is over. The point is that even the most level-headed of adults can seriously lose focus in a crisis.

4 Learning from Adults' Experience

The ideas in this section are applicable to all adults in a close relationship with children – parents, of course, but also children's key person in their early years provision and other familiar adults in nurseries, primary schools and out-of-school provision.

Step-by-step coaching

Coaching is a positive framework for approaching how adults can support children's learning of any lifeskills, especially those in which there are safety implications. The idea of coaching children is also positive because it locates adult expertise in particular areas, rather than promoting an image of adults who always know more than the children. As girls and boys grow older, they soon have areas of expertise, knowledge and skills that they can in turn share with the familiar adults in their life. The relationship of coaching, skill-sharing and exchange of knowledge can become a pleasurable two-way process.

The essence of coaching, so that children can learn as well as possible, has been summed up as 'tell–show–do'.

■ *Tell* children what you are doing and explain why, as and when this is appropriate. Describe your actions in words and phrases that are simple enough for these children. Be prepared to explain again or several times, if necessary.

- *Show* children clearly what you mean through demonstration. Children need to see how to do something and be able to make a clear link between what you say and do.
- Give children an opportunity to *do* it themselves, as soon as you have completed 'tell' and 'show'. Encourage them to ask for help as and when they want. Offer guidance as they wish.

Children need plenty of active, hands-on practice and that adults handle any mistakes with good humour and understanding. For many skills this practice will be graded step by step, and children will move on to more challenging skills as they get older. Repeat the sequence in response to what children need in terms of more explanation, demonstration or guided practice.

Children learn best when they feel able to ask for assistance, confident that adults will be a genuinely helpful resource.

- Respond to children's requests as promptly as possible and in the way that they ask. Sometimes they may want physical help in managing something too heavy for them. On other occasions they may appreciate new information or reminders.
- Consider whether it will be helpful to create something visual, with the active involvement of the children. A set of photos, ideally featuring children and adults from this provision, can be organised with simple wording. This visual prompt can be in the format of a wall display or a little booklet – whichever makes sense.
- Encourage a child to think through a plan or possibilities. But do not insist that they work it out alone with minimal direction when their body language shows that they are struggling and will give up if no help is forthcoming.
- When there is a real safety issue, adults need to offer a firm suggestion, but this can still be done in a respectful way to children. It would be irresponsible for practitioners or parents to allow children to experience injury as the direct consequence of how they are using a tool or behaving in a potentially unsafe situation, such as close to a road.

Children flourish with encouraging and accurate feedback. They learn from 'well done', with a specific mention of what they have managed so far. This kind of feedback also acknowledges when children had the sense to come and ask for more help and/or another explanation. Warm words help a child to persevere or to try another method: 'You've done really well so far, let's see how you've got stuck here' or 'I can see you're frustrated, let's see if it will work this way.' Children are also encouraged by appropriate compliments from adults such as: 'I'm so pleased I can trust you all to do this on your own' or 'Good idea! I've never thought of doing it this way.' Children do not benefit from indiscriminate praise: being told something is 'brilliant' when they know things have not gone right.

Be clear about technique and safety

No adult was born knowing how to crack an egg or use sharp scissors appropriately. Anyone is a better coach when they become more conscious of how they approach and carry out simple everyday tasks.

- Is there a best way to prepare for this task? A recipe for cooking will usually give a sequence of steps. Generally it is wise to follow the recipe first before trying the 'bit of this, bit of that' approach.
- If there is a mending task, like a torn book, are there some materials that have to be prepared first in order for the task to work?
- Be ready to break down a task into steps that are as basic as the children need. Younger children or those with learning disabilities may need finer steps than others, so that they can learn and find satisfaction in what they achieve.
- Set a good example to the children by explaining the practical reasons for doing a task in a particular way. Why does this technique work better than another one?
- Do some techniques incur more risk than others, physical or with the possibility that a lot of hard work will come to nothing? Explain simply the 'how' and 'why' to children: 'You need to glue this bit first, then you fix it onto the other part' or 'You need to hold the bowl firmly or else it may tip.'
- It will not be long before the slightly older children repeat these simple explanations and instructions as they assist younger or less able children.

Children can learn about any safety implications when patient adults take them through the process of tell–show–do. Helpful adults voice out loud to children what they are doing, so that the safety messages become explicit through words as well as adult action. Children need to be active in doing and not only listening, so ensure that they can take part in the activity. They may listen very carefully for a while, but children soon need to get their hands on materials and tools.

Without going on and on about safety issues, adults can reinforce the safety message when they are doing something in a deliberate way. Explanatory phrases might be, 'Do you see that I always strike the match away from myself. That's so I never get the flame close to my body'; or 'It's important that I put my other hand here when I'm cutting the sandwiches with the knife. If I put it here (brief demonstration) I might cut my fingers.' Opportunities should be taken as they arise to be explicit about safety. Avoid losing children's attention through excessive repetition or by harping on possible dangers. Phrases like, 'I might burn myself' are less practical than, 'This is a good way to hold the handle of our pot, because it gets very hot closer to the pan.'

It is a wise adult habit to read instructions out loud, even for something that is very familiar. Children are then alerted to the helpful role of instructions, many of which will have a visual component when they are younger. Children learn that checking how to make this model or work this simple machine is a sensible first step. They will be able to use this route as well as ask for adult help if they get confused. There is also a valuable early literacy message for younger children that there are many good reasons why it is handy to be able to read.

Children can learn a great deal through discovery, but it is unhelpful to leave them to reinvent the wheel when there are tried and tested ways to undertake an activity. Helpful adults share useful tips and techniques on how to do a practical activity. Good technique is also likely to be safer as well as leading to a more satisfying end-product for children. Possibilities include, 'It works better if you do little sawing movements like this' or 'This kind of sewing goes up and down again into the material. It doesn't go over the side.' It is possible to acknowledge with a keen young cook, 'I can see you're planning some creative cooking without a recipe. I'll be interested to have a taste when your cake is made.'

In the woodland with Stocksfield Avenue Nursery

This group of young children go once a week into the same area as part of a joint project with Sightlines Initiative. All the adults are attentive towards the safety of the children but enable them to take risks appropriate for their age. For these young girls and boys the walk down through the woodland was as important and interesting as the final destination. Children took their time and accepted help for clambering if they wished.

They reached an area of the woodland that was further than they had ever gone up to now. Once on the flatter sections around a stream, children had time to get a sense of their surroundings, this newly encountered space within the woodland. They chose to stand and look, some individuals longer than others, before moving into the different parts and start 'adventuring', as the Sightlines team describe it.

Some children became interested in the water of the stream and discovered it was quite cold. Others were interested in getting out into the stream a bit by using the rocks. By the end of the morning visit, one or two children had become very adept at moving along the edge of the stream using rocks as a series of stepping platforms. The skills were partly physical – movement and balance were crucial – but the children also judged what they could manage and assessed their own risk. There was no danger; the worst that happened was a couple of wet feet.

Several children became interested in twigs and bits of greenery in the stream and explored throwing in items. They watched how the items went with the flow, sometimes got stuck and whether they could be dislodged by children throwing a well-positioned stone. There was a great deal of conversation around what and

how and maybe. Children also took time to observe the consequences of their actions before the next decision.

A number of children become engaged in throwing stones into the stream and at one point were busy finding and moving across quite large stones and rocks, which they wanted one adult to heave into the middle of the stream.

One boy and then a second worked out how to move past some fallen branches and reach another flat area just slightly upstream. They explored that section and soon several other children could see them (they were only a very short distance) and these boys and girls talked, looked and worked out how to reach that other part. These children could still be easily seen by the adults and one moved across to be with them in this new and interesting part of the stream.

5 Active in Nurture and Personal Routines

Early years provision, school or out-of-school settings have the potential to offer plenty of opportunities for children to learn to share in their own care and personal routines. But children are also keen to help out in the more general domestic routines to ensure that things run smoothly, whether that be in a group provision or a family home. Young children who feel emotionally secure themselves are also ready to be caring towards other children: their peers and younger ones.

Care of babies and younger ones

Practitioners working with babies and very young children are directly responsible for their personal care and safety. But it is possible for nursery practitioners, childminders or nannies to welcome slightly older children alongside as friendly company and guided helpers. Over twos are often fascinated by the care of babies or toddlers, keen to be an assistant and intrigued to hear that they too were once so little and vulnerable.

- Slightly older children can watch at changing or feeding time. Sensitive practitioners will notice if the baby does not welcome the company. In that case the explanation might be, 'If it's more than just me, Natasha gets distracted from her bottle.'
- Continue to give the baby plenty of attention and include her or him with eye contact when talking with the watching child about the routine. A young boy or girl will be interested in, 'I need to clean

Jasmin's bottom so she doesn't get sore' or 'We need to have Stevie's bottles extra-special clean, because babies easily get an upset stomach.'

■ Be ready to answer children's questions, for instance about the disposable gloves worn at changing time in nursery. Keep the explanation simple, 'My special gloves make sure I don't pass on any germs to Jasmin, or between the babies.' Perhaps explain further that babies can get ill easily, if 'we aren't extra careful'.

■ Of course, early years practitioners never delegate changing or feeding to an older child; the adult remains responsible. However, slightly older children can look and learn, hand over the cream or a new nappy.

■ Children are often adept at keeping a baby amused. They may imitate the way adults communicate with babies – the circling, repetitive pattern of infant-directed speech that holds babies' attention – or copy gentle stroking motions on the baby's hand. Children may like to choose items of clothing when the baby needs a clean outfit.

Older, disabled children, who continue to need support in care, are more likely to want privacy especially during intimate routines like toileting. But it will always be for the children to say or indicate that they would like more company than just the adult. Disabled children who need regular physical support through exercises can sometimes feel that this special time does not make them feel positively special, because they are isolated from other children in the group.

Possibilities in your provision

It may seem more feasible for childminders or nannies to involve older children in the personal routines of babies. In a family setting it can be very normal that older siblings become safely involved in the care of younger ones. Children whose childcare is in age-grouped nursery provision can lose out on this area of experience. But this situation is not inevitable. Rather than saying 'We can't do that', some early years teams have considered ways to welcome the safe involvement of older children (Lindon, 2006).

■ Some group settings make it easy for the slightly older children to 'visit' the baby and toddler room. This possibility may have evolved from siblings who want to see 'my baby'. But often it becomes clear that quite a few over twos or threes are interested in spending some time with much younger children.

■ Within a long day in nursery there is often a period of time when younger ones are in the company of slightly older boys and girls, indoors or outside. Sometimes this section of the day is a practical response to much reduced numbers in the early morning or later afternoon.

- Babies and toddlers also like and need the company of older children. Attentive adults can ensure any safety issues are addressed – in nursery as within a family home. Older threes and fours often become actively helpful with statements such as, 'The babies are coming; we need to put away the toys with little bits.'
- Let parents know about the change, if bringing the age groups together is an innovation in a previously age-segregated nursery. It is possible to explain by written communication (newsletter, email, parents' board or website) as well as face-to-face conversation.

Integrating children of different ages

Apart from their development work with the Forest School, the team of the Children's Centre at Bridgwater College have been active in blurring the artificial boundary between 'care' and 'education'. In a visit for the first edition of this book it was possible to observe innovatory practice which has subsequently become more common across early years provision.

The team made the decision to encourage contact between babies and toddlers and the slightly older children. So, while the under-twos had an area of the centre that was especially organised for their needs, the three- and four-year-olds were able to join them easily. A quiet room where babies, or other children, can sleep was also the location for peaceable activities such as exploratory play with a treasure basket or other collections of materials.

During my visit, I saw two four-year-olds entertaining a child under one year who was sitting in a low baby chair. The older children were talking with the baby and helping her to play with some suitable beads. One of the older children then helped the baby out of her bib and, with the support of a practitioner, out of the chair onto the ground to crawl. (Adults are always close.) In the same general area, some older children were working with dough on a table and another baby crawled across. Supported by leaning against the adult's knee, this baby watched with interest and then started to squeeze some dough of his own.

Hygiene and cleanliness

Of course, it is practitioners' responsibility to maintain standards of hygiene and healthy conditions. However, children can learn the basics of how to keep themselves healthy at a young age. They are reasonably willing to cooperate with what familiar adults ask of them in a friendly way and if they are allowed time to follow a request. Early childhood is the best period to start to build healthy habits for hygiene and also over food. Familiar adults always have to set a good example, to behave in ways that children will then imitate. Younger children develop habits because 'it's what we do here'. Older children are more likely to continue with healthy habits when adults have taken the trouble to explain the 'why' of underlying patterns of good hygiene such as hand-washing.

Encouraging healthy habits

Familiar adults will wash the hands of babies and toddlers, but two- and three-year-olds are ready to wash their own hands, with friendly reminders as necessary. Those reminders may be spoken words but can also be visual reminders from photos with simple written words. These notices, placed in the bathroom or elsewhere, are best made with the children's help and with the children featured in the photos still attending this provision.

The plethora of cleaning products in the market, including anti-bacterial ones, has sometimes obscured the fact that simple habits of hygiene are highly effective. A considerable number of food-poisoning incidents, both domestic and commercial, arise from the direct contamination of food by adults who have not washed their hands after going to the toilet. So there is good reason to explain the importance of hand-washing to children, rather than risk the impression that it is just one more thing about which grown-ups like to make a fuss.

- Find a simple way to explain why it is important for everyone to wash their hands after going to the toilet. Establish the habit that everyone washes their hands before handling food, either to eat a meal or to do some cooking together.
- It is unwise to give young children the impression that normal life is full of dangerous germs or other substances ready to make them very sick. A practical explanation may involve not getting earth from the garden or bits of play dough into everyone's food. Children can understand this idea because they can see sand or paint on their hands.
- Explain the simple idea that some things are fine where they belong in our bodies. But they can sometimes make us ill or cause trouble elsewhere, as the two examples that follow show.

For instance, 'pee' and 'poo', or whatever words the children use, are what is left over when 'our bodies have taken all the goodness out of our food'. Young children can begin to understand that everyone's body needs to get rid of what is left, but the waste products are not 'dirty' and neither is the child. However, 'pee' and 'poo' are a concentrated version of what the body does not want and cannot use. So, it is never a good idea to put it back in again by sucking unwashed fingers, nor to pass it into food that will then be eaten.

The idea that some things are alright where they belong in the body is also a useful way to explain to little girls why they should wipe their bottom from front to back. Familiar adults will know the risk of conditions like thrush but will need to explain it to them in a very simple way. This could be done by perhaps saying that there are 'good things' that live in everyone's digestive system (or the general 'tummy') that help to absorb what the body needs from food, but that the waste, when expelled, can make girls sore if it happens to get into the vagina. Use words that make sense to young children. And as for any wise adult guidance, practitioners or parents will always need a ready answer to a child's 'why?'

Keeping clean enough

Standards of hygiene matter, but it is possible for adults to become obsessive about hand-washing. There are serious disadvantages for young children if issues of 'not clean enough' are used as an excuse to reduce children's time outdoors. If young children are to enjoy the natural environment of a garden or local outdoor spaces, their hands and other parts of their body in warmer weather, as well as their clothes, will get temporarily grubby.

Projects to get young children into woodland areas all address possible concerns around dirt and cleanliness, as well broader issues of safety and risk. These initiatives include those within the Forest School approach (examples in Lindon, 2009b and 2010), the Reggio-inspired approach of Sightlines Initiative and the Nature Kindergarten concept developed in Scotland by Claire Warden (2010 and www.mindstretchers.co.uk/nature-kindergartens.html). The common approach is to accept that part of an enjoyable time for children and adults in the outdoors is that everyone will get fairly messy and grubby by the end of a visit, especially in winter or after rain.

Appropriate clothing for the weather is a practical issue. But partnership with parents needs to address that young children need suitable clothes for play in the garden, even if they are not taken on local outings to woodland. Natural substances largely brush off and shoes or boots can be cleaned. Practitioners can express understanding for any parents who are keen that their children look smart or fashionable. However, continued communication needs to establish that active play is the pattern here, with time outdoors. Children will use their hands to steady themselves when they clamber, they may slide over (intentionally or not) when there are mud slides, and they need to feel it is fine to gather wood, leaves, stones and other natural materials. Attentive familiar adults ensure that children do not put unsuitable materials in their mouth – either through inattention or because children are still very young.

Practitioners involved in outdoors experiences, or the fully outdoors provision like the Nature Kindergartens, need to commit to the crucial basics of hygiene that children are able to clean their hands after going to the toilet – which may be an outdoors toilet or a designated tree. They also need the means to clean their hands properly before eating a snack or picnic lunch in the woodland. In many locations there will be no running tap water. The Mindstretchers kindergarten teams take water in a camping canister and use biodegradable soap. Some outdoor project teams also take wet wipes, sometimes anti-bacterial, although there are some concerns about allergies or over-use of anti-bacterial products.

Germs and keeping well

The adult task is to help children develop an appropriate wariness about germs without making them feel unclean or frightened. Some general rules need to be communicated.

- Germs or 'bugs' can easily be passed on to someone else and make them ill. Even a cold is not much fun to have and some illnesses are much worse.
- Putting a hand in front of the mouth, for a sneeze or a cough, stops anyone shooting germs straight out for someone else to breathe.
- For the same reason, everyone blows their nose into a tissue, rather than wiping it on a sleeve or elsewhere and puts tissues in the bin.

Look for opportunities, especially if children make a relevant comment, to explain that not all health problems are 'catching'. Children with eczema and other skin irritations sometimes have to cope with their peers' belief that eczema is a kind of 'lergy' which can be passed on by contact. Without a simple explanation, young children may think that some disabling conditions experienced by children are contagious. Under these circumstances, children are not being intentionally cruel or foolish; they simply do not have the information base to know better.

A similar explanation about transfer of dirt or germs is also important if children are to play a safe part in the care of animals. The same habit of hand-washing applies after cuddling the family cat or stroking the nursery hamster. Domestic pets roll in the dirt or clean their fur after licking their bottom, and these bits should not go into anyone's mouth. The same high standard needs to be taken, and explained to children, if they are taken to visit farms that welcome nursery or school trips. Any setting of this kind should have easily accessible facilities for hand-washing. However, the adults accompanying young children are responsible for ensuring that facilities are used, especially before snack-time. It is also important to recognise how much young children put their hands up to their mouth, even if they do not suck thumbs of fingers.

Basic first aid

The prime responsibility for first aid rests with adults, especially with under-fives. Of course this attention means that familiar adults should be comfortable with physical contact. No practitioner can meet their duty of care in provision with a deeply misguided no-touch policy.

Even familiar adults should not impose first aid on children without warning and concern for the children's feelings. Show respect to even the youngest of children by telling them what needs to be done. Listen to and acknowledge their feelings and fears. Never tell them something 'doesn't hurt' when their words or expression says clearly that it does cause pain. Likewise it is very unwise to reassure children that, 'This won't hurt' when there is a good chance that it will. Better to warn with, 'This will sting a bit' or 'This isn't going to be comfortable. But I'll be quick'. Then there are opportunities to offer comfort and say 'Well done'.

As children get a little older, they can be more active in the nurture offered through appropriate and timely first aid.

- Invite them to help in their own care – to clean their knee or work on a splinter, with adult guidance. Older children may appreciate being given the choice as a signal that they are capable. But they may still prefer that a trusted adult does the first aid – even grown-ups sometimes like some direct help.

- Look for safe opportunities for children to help the adults when they recognise the need for some first aid. Perhaps a child, who has washed her hands, as she knows is important, can hand over a plaster.
- Be ready to follow children's advice, learned from what they have been told. Perhaps a child will tell her key person to 'sit down and get that splinter out right now' or suggest that his childminder sits quiet for a moment 'because you banged your head hard on that cupboard door'.
- If children are curious about an existing injury, answer their questions. Explain simply what happened to a child who asks about a personal injury – cut, bruise or burn. Bring in another child with courtesy when the question is about a third party.

It is constructive to look for ways to let older children and those in school or out-of-school provision be part of the record keeping that has to follow an accident. If they understand the adult obligation and responsibility to record, there is less chance that children will believe an accident book is a record of who has been 'bad' or 'whose fault it was'. Try to make children a constructive part of the conversation that needs to happen with a parent at the end of the day or session when there has been an accident or injury.

Fire, heat and safety issues

Everyone needs to develop a healthy respect for and care around fire and heat. Of course, uncontrolled fire or heat poses a significant safety issue for both children and adults. Many children are injured in burn or scald incidents in family homes and some are killed in house fires. However, there has been an unfortunate trend to remove children from any contact with heat or fire.

The outdoors movement has been part of reversing that excessive caution, but some practitioners still err towards decisions that are risk averse. Not every provision has easy access to a kitchen for proper cooking but, even with facilities, some practitioners still restrict themselves to cold-cooking activities. Of course, young children should not be left alone with lit candles. But they will never learn to be safe if, in the name of health and safety, there are only pretend candles on a birthday cake or crinkled red paper for Diwali diva lamps. There is still sometimes an audible intake of breath in workshops when a participant describes activities with children where they have lit candles, for instance for Advent, on a birthday cake or for the pleasure of watching the soft light against the backdrop of a dark winter afternoon.

However, an increasing range of early years, school and out-of-school teams have realised that childhood is the time to show children how to behave safely around sources of heat or flame. These are the years when boys and girls are likely to listen to words of warning and practical advice from trusted adults. It is the time to establish, as far as possible, secure habits for how to behave sensibly. Children who are excessively protected from fire may become so intrigued that they experiment in ways that create serious danger for themselves and others. Older children and young adolescents may be genuinely ignorant of the risks of an uncontrolled fire in dry woodland or indulge in dangerous behaviour, such as throwing aerosols onto a bonfire.

Safe behaviour with fire

Teams involved in outdoors projects frequently make time for coaching children through managed experiences: of making and tending to a fire, say, or the different ways of enjoying outdoor cooking.

In the Forest School at Bridgwater, practitioners build children's secure understanding about fire over a period of months. Adults steadily teach them about collecting suitable material for the bonfire, how to light fires and contain them, safety close to the bonfire and cooking on the open fire – this even with their youngest visitors: three- and four-year-olds from the children's centre.

First hand experiences enable children to not only understand the potential danger of fire, but also how to treat this valuable resource with respect. All the children, young and old, are shown how to approach the fire carefully and to maintain a safe distance from it. The Bridgwater approach is to sit on the ring of logs set around the fire. The adults as well as the children always approach the fire from behind the log seats, then step over and sit down. The same pattern is followed in reverse when anyone leaves the fire area, whether or not the fire is burning at the time.

Children learn how to cook snacks safely from the distance of held sticks and are part of the activity to find a stick that is 'this long' and 'this thick' (shown by adults). So, over a period of time, within the context of visits to the woodlands, children hear practical explanations alongside demonstration and opportunities for active practice.

Apart from the evidence of how children have learned about fire within the forest itself, the team have at least one example of how this understanding was generalised by a child. In one four-year-old child's home, a burning coal fell from the living-room fire. The young boy calmly tipped a cup of water over the coal while the adults were still staring at it. When asked how he knew what to do, the boy just replied confidently, 'Oh, Forest School'.

Using fire and heat can be an emotive issue and some practitioners feel that it is absolutely off limits. There needs to be a full discussion in a team about how experiences will be organised and communicated to families. Similar reflection, but usually without the colleague discussion, is also relevant for childminders. Look at possibilities for outdoors experience of fire, for instance, there are ways to cook in a garden on a small or contained fire, or with a one-use barbecue box rather than the open adult version. Practical suggestions are available in the section about fire in Claire Warden (2007), and ideas and materials in the 'Cooking Outdoors' section in www.mindstretchers.co.uk/cat/C.html and the Viking Ware section of Inside-Out Nature in www.insideoutnature.co.uk

Emergency procedures and drills

Every early years, playwork or school setting needs a clear and well-understood procedure for unexpected emergencies. Adults have a major responsibility, but safe evacuation also depends on experiences that have enabled the children to understand what they have to do.

- Children need to play an active part in safety drills. Help them to understand what is happening, how and why, rather than giving them a sense that, in the event of an emergency, adults will take over every aspect of directing children.
- Talk with children about the drill, explaining that it is one of those things that will probably never happen, but is best that everyone knows what to do and how to behave in case it does.
- Practise regularly and give children constructive feedback about what went well and what could be improved.
- Model calm and prompt behaviour, taking the practice drill seriously so that children will follow the adult example.

Emergency procedures are not only relevant for the evacuation of buildings or an area of the outdoor space of fixed provision. Adults and children also need to know and understand, at an appropriate level, how to behave under sudden changes of circumstance during local outings or regular outdoors trips. For instance, part of the outdoors experience is to be robust about a wide range of weather. Yet there are some weather conditions, such as a thunderstorm or heavy mist, when there needs to be urgent rethinking. Young children need to understand that they may have to move back into the central area or base camp of an outdoor project. Much older children or adolescents need to have been thoroughly trained in how to behave for safety under extreme conditions, before they are encouraged to venture out in small groups for independent treks.

6 Physical Play and Exploration

Children need challenge and excitement. If their play environment is devoid of any adventurous activities – removed in the name of safety – children may slump into inactive and unenthusiastic patterns of play. Alternatively a proportion of children will discover ways to spice up their play environment. They will ensure that boring grown-ups do not catch them playing energetic games which attract adult disapproval.

Children can put themselves at unnecessary risk if they rush at forbidden climbing or jumping in order to complete their enjoyment while they are temporarily out of sight or earshot. In contrast, children who know they have time and adult encouragement do not have to be secretive and speedy. They are confident of engaging in activities that give them the chance to judge how fast, high or wobbly. Adults are a source of help, if wanted, and encouragement to children to stretch their current skills (see Lindon 2010, 2011 for examples).

A safe enough environment

Every setting needs to consider the balance between safety and a decent level of challenge in physical play, as well as exciting activities that stretch children intellectually and emotionally. Growing concern about the consequences of over-protection has led to much more discussion around creating a safe environment in which children, even young ones, can take risks and learn to assess their own level of risk for more adventurous play.

- Find alternatives to saying 'no' and go instead for the possibilities of saying, 'yes, so long as…'. Very young children and toddlers want and need to use their physical skills, so watch out for bad habits, of adults saying 'no' without real consideration.

- It is possible to keep very young children safe through friendly supervision, often achieved by playing with them.

- Ensure a soft or yielding surface for children's landing from leaps or somersaults. A low-impact surface in a play area can reduce bumps and bruises. But watch out for children who then think that a safety surface means they are protected from the consequences of truly reckless behaviour. Foam mats can be brought out for crawling–chasing games and safe wrestling activities with toddlers.

- Use natural opportunities to explore rules with the children for a situation that needs some limits. Everyone probably cannot get on the climbing frame at the same time. With a bit of adult help even young children manage to wait for their turn on the milk crate or the large-blocks obstacle course which they have helped construct. Older children understand why there is a system of one-at-a-time on the swinging rope in the adventure playground.

- A necessary 'no' or 'not like that' needs to be followed by a discussion of the alternatives. Children who behave in an unsafe way with age-appropriate equipment or resources need the experience of adults who are willing to problem-solve rather than simply treat children as the problem.

Deciding on resources that always need an adult

When children ask 'why' about safety rules, they deserve a proper answer. The reply is neither the confrontational, 'because we say so' nor the weak, other-blaming of, 'because we're not allowed to let you do that'.

Sometimes responsible adults decide that a particular activity or experience needs an accompanying adult. For instance, there may always be a playworker at the very top of the big slide in the adventure playground. Each child is offered help, if so desired, to get onto their mat and the adult ensures that the previous child has cleared the bottom of the slide before the next child starts.

The team at The Rainbow Centre (Marham) are committed to offering children plenty of time outdoors in their well-resourced garden areas. They have made a considered decision about a few resources that are only available when an adult is part of the group. For instance, a water system with a pump and barrels has a notice that explains simply that an adult must always be around when children want to play with the equipment. However, that adult behaves as a supportive play companion, fully involved in the children's current interests about the water, and certainly not as an impersonal supervisor. The equipment has been designed so that children can operate the pumps themselves.

Learning to assess risk

It is important that children learn to assess and take manageable risks. Adults can take good care of children and still allow them a wide range of opportunities to decide on the risk level themselves, rather than always having to say 'yes' or 'no'.

- Let the children say out loud how high they want to go and what help they would welcome. Children will learn about safe footing and judging a good jumping height. Adult-friendly involvement can empower a child to stay within their own comfort zone. Children need to feel confident enough to say, 'I don't want to do that' or 'I don't want to go so high as Teja'.
- Supportive adults make considered decisions about when to encourage a child who is regularly reluctant to take minor risks. A possible compromise might be, 'How about you try a jump from down here' or 'I can hold your hand as you balance. Would you like that?'

Honest adults make a clear distinction between their concerns and those felt by children. There is a difference between saying, 'I'm concerned that's a bit too high for you' and the rather sneaky approach of, 'Don't you think that's too high for you?' A confident child may fairly answer the second comment with a 'No', and then what does the adults do next? A more straightforward adult can follow up the first comment with, 'I'd be grateful if you'd do a few jumps from here first.' It is important, of course, that practitioners are self-aware, and support colleagues, if some adults are fearful and so restrict children unduly. The overall aim is to talk about safety issues with children and listen to their views as sensible fellow human beings who happen to be younger.

Building with milk crates

During the morning of my visit to Grandpont Nursery School, the children had designed and built a channel to bring water from the outdoor tap to their sandpit. Lengths of firm plastic guttering had been supported by milk crates in a plan discussed and put into practice entirely by the children, who had not needed to ask for any adult help with this enterprise.

There had been an open discussion with the children, especially about the height of the construction using milk crates. Practitioners were ready to have brief conversations and demonstrate for instance that, 'We don't climb on the crates if they are more than two high. Because it's very wobbly, like this...' They heard children involved in the construction discussing with each other the features of their building. Children recalled the limits they felt were fair and decided that, 'if we want to climb on them, we'll make it long and not high'.

With some children, the adult aim is to boost confidence and encourage an uneasy child to try something that is slightly challenging. The best way to help is with a one-step-at-at-time approach and by showing respect for individual children's concerns or reservations.

It is possible to explore a personalised safe challenge zone with individual girls and boys and help them with a gentle push to move their skills and confidence that little bit further. A familiar adult can encourage with, 'Try a step higher' or, 'Hold on to that rope for another count of 1, 2, 3. You did it!' The challenge for children is not always about large physical movements. Some children just need that gentle push with, 'I reckon you can do this jigsaw, if I just start you with the edges' or, 'Would you like to hold Timmy Cat (a soft toy) while you tell your story?'

Constructive feedback offers positive descriptions to the child, such as, 'Well done for jumping from the higher step', even if this was a much lower step than that managed by the child's peers. Feedback ceases to be constructive if it is undermined with a message of, 'Why were you worried in the first place?' It is disrespectful of children if their caution gets them labelled as 'over-anxious' or 'clingy'.

Assessing individual risk

Kidsactive (now part of KIDS) starts from a commitment to the right of all children to play. At the time of my visit, their London adventure play facility often took children who had experienced difficulty in other play settings. The adventure playground was an inclusive setting that met the needs of disabled children, but also welcomed siblings and local children who did not live with a disability.

An individual risk assessment was made for some children, starting with issues closely related to a child's disability (for instance frailty or likelihood of losing balance) or challenging behaviour (such as running off or eating inappropriate substances). The level of risk was assessed as significant, moderate or low. Plans were then made to manage the risk so that the child was enabled to play and enjoy the setting.

The management of the individual risk was sometimes related to specialist equipment, but more often was through appropriate adult support and attention within a setting with a high adult-to-child ratio. The team were of the view that experience of acceptable risk was a positive addition to the children's environment, not something to avoid, and that disabled children need to have the normal tumbles of childhood.

1, 2, 3 – where are you?

The Forest School at Bridgwater approaches outdoor physical safety skills through step-by-step learning. As well as exploring the nature of the forest environment with children, the team supports children in understanding what to do if they lose sight of their friends. They explain how to reply loudly to an adult call of 'Where are you?'

Early in the children's sequence of visits they all play the '1, 2, 3 – where are you?' game. This approach is taken in some Forest School projects. The adults disappear into the nearby trees and bushes – not far away – and the children have to find them by calling out '1, 2, 3 – where are you?' The hidden adults reply and the children locate them using the sounds. Hiding and finding games continue as part of the woodland experience.

Children are allowed to explore at their own pace. If they want to hold hands, they can, but they are not required to hang on tight to friends or adults. When children are confident to move independently within the woodland, they are welcome to roam. The Bridgwater area is secure and bounded by a fence that the children explore during their early visits. Adults shadow children from a short distance so that no child is ever out of hearing or sight and children can easily get help or advice when they want. Although some children have enjoyed wandering off on their own, no child has ever got lost or gone beyond the fenced area.

Other woodland projects have operated in more open areas of woodland. The outdoor teams then reach an agreement with children about the boundaries within which they can roam and use visual markers to show them the limits. For trips further afield, children are always accompanied by an adult.

7 Practical Lifeskills

Adults who are undertaking a practical activity with young children need to make a balanced assessment of possible risks, determining sensible levels of supervision and, in group settings, an appropriate child-to-adult ratio for this experience. Many activities can be broken down into their separate steps so that children can learn safely. In any group provision, there should be enough practitioners so that a team member can be part of a sustained activity, like cooking. Children involved in the activity have the continued support of the same person and other children, who are not currently involved, still have adults as play and conversational companions.

Being a participant and guide in an activity enables adults – parents as well as practitioners – to talk about and show useful safety tips and techniques within context, as the experience unfolds. Young children learn best how to use a cheese grater when they have one in their hand, along with the cheese for the recipe for cheese straws or for one possible filling in their sandwich. The same principle applies for learning safe use of a screwdriver or a garden rake.

Children have many years in which to learn all the skills that will support them as competent adults. However, even the youngest ones will learn in small steps along the way. Children grasp some skills fairly quickly. For other skills, adults need to monitor carefully how much the children can manage and the extent to which they need a grown-up to be closely involved. There can and should be many opportunities for learning that lie between the one extreme of never allowing children to do anything that is remotely risky and the other extreme of handing over the electric drill along with the chip pan.

It is helpful to consider possible activities, even for the youngest children, along a continuing line of the decreasing involvement of an adult guide in line with the children's increasing ability to take responsibility. There are five general steps on this continuum:

1. Adults do the activity/task entirely for the children, keeping the children away. Either the children cannot be involved or adults judge that it is not safe for them to be, however much they want to help by doing part of the activity.
2. Adults remain basically in charge of the activity, but encourage the children to join in safely, in an agreed way, and by watching and listening to the adult. Children are not left alone, even for a moment. They are thanked for their help, even if their assistance was limited, for the pleasure of their company and possibly for handy reminders of what the adult should do next.
3. Adults now encourage children to have a go and use skills that they have practised. The grown-up – practitioner or parent – remains very close and ready to offer help or advice as soon as a child asks for it.
4. It is now time for adults to delegate the task to the children, trusting them to complete it without supervision. Adults are still available if children want help but they are allowed to get on with the task without close supervision. As appropriate, the adult is ready to check on the completed task and to offer constructive, encouraging feedback and any tips. Be pleased with them.
5. The task is completely within the children's area of responsibility. Adults neither remind nor ask them about it. However, those adults do take the time to compliment children and show that their skills are not taken for granted.

Bear these steps in mind as you look at the areas that follow.

Using tools

In many craft activities, real tools work better and so are safer in the end than 'safe' child versions. Slightly smaller tools are sometimes easier for smaller hands and some adjustments may be necessary for physically disabled children to manipulate tools to their satisfaction.

Early years, school and out-of-school settings, who have addressed the learning issues involved in using tools, are consistent in saying that greater hazards arise from children trying to make inadequate tools work. Blunt knives, saws or scissors can be wielded with so much force to try to make them do the job, that even careful children can lose their grip. Plastic is rarely, if ever, the best material to choose for working tools.

Children's satisfaction is also greatly reduced when, despite their best efforts, they cannot produce what they wanted. Toy companies are energetic in promoting plastic children's versions of tools, but these sets are not worth buying when ordinary tools are available to do the job. The time to consider a well-made pretend version is for activities that are way beyond the safe zone for young children, such as handling power tools.

Learning to use tools is a process, like so many of the skills that children gain, and not a one-off event. Adults help when they are patient and:

- show children how to hold and use a tool
- demonstrate techniques to children in how best to make tools do the job
- demonstrate and reinforce through conversation how to move around when carrying a tool – mainly with the point downwards
- tell–show–do about the responsible storage of tools, both how to put them down temporarily and how all tools are stored in the particular setting or family home
- decide if any of the tools are just for the adults in the setting and explain to the children the reasons why.

Practitioners need to be able to explain clearly to uneasy parents and to an inspector or advisor the steps they take to ensure safe use of tools. A considerable amount of this appropriate adult effort will lie in undertaking the active opportunities described in the list above. Supportive adult behaviour also includes 'well done' for safe use, reminders when necessary and a calm, 'Stop, look at what you are about to do' when intervention is necessary. Sometimes it will make sense to have a reminder visual about how to be safe and at other times a whole group may benefit from a recap on, 'How do we...?'

Some practitioners and teams experience high levels of pressure to demonstrate their level of care over safety to somebody else. Putting up photos to show how to hold and use every possible tool may not help keep children entirely safe. Providing first hand experiences, so that children actually learn this behaviour, might be rather more useful. Similar to keeping written risk assessment to an effective level, there are disadvantages to plastering a setting with photos or cartoon illustrations on 'how to be safe'. When practitioners are pushed to over-doing such visuals, they simply become wallpaper, with children no longer looking at them or being unimpressed about forever being asked to check the picture.

Cooking

Learning to cook is a valuable lifeskill as well as a potential source of great satisfaction to children. Even very young children can be proud of the ginger biscuits or pizza dough that they have made.

- Choose the simpler recipes to start with, but look for opportunities to make real food that transforms through the cooking process.
- Share techniques with children such as weighing, cutting, spooning and pouring. Show them how to hold a knife and place their hands for safe cutting.
- If children can be with an adult in the kitchen, explain to and show them how to deal safely with heat, including how to hold the handle of a pan and put on oven gloves and give reasons why.
- Let children do as much as possible. The time will come when they can guide the adult in answer to, 'What should I do now?' (the answer might be, 'Wash your hands'), or 'What's the matter with this?' (the answer might be, 'Push the pan handles so that they do not stick out').
- Find ways for children to be part of the tidying and washing up that completes a cooking or food preparation activity. It is wise to establish the habit for children that everyone helps out and that clearing up is not something to delegate to the grown-ups.
- Children can also enjoy what follows from the enjoyment of cooking or food preparation, such as making rolls or sandwiches with a choice of fillings. Good food deserves a nicely-laid-out table and friends who sit down to enjoy the meal or snack.

Access to the kitchen

Some group settings have a policy that children should never enter the kitchen. Sometimes this restriction is the interpretation they are given of welfare requirements. Undoubtedly, it would not be safe to have young children wandering in and out of a nursery kitchen, or to have them present when the kitchen team is busy producing a considerable number of lunches. Group provision is different from a home kitchen used by a childminder or nanny, or by parents at home with their own children. However, there are ways to help children get cooking as much as possible and to understand something of safe behaviour in the kitchen.

- Some teams arrange supervised visits of a small number of children to the nursery kitchen at quiet times of the day. These visits are often to take their jam tarts or little cakes in to be cooked.

- It can be possible for children and an adult to gather and weigh ingredients and follow the recipe for scones right up to the point where they are oven-ready.
- Practitioners can work jointly with parents who are willing to cook with their children at home. Informative displays, for example, can show through photos and words how a particular group of children found out about and made real bread. The display is completed with a little pocket with copies of the recipe for parents.
- Some larger nurseries and children's centres have a real equipped kitchen in one corner of a large space. This facility is in regular use throughout the day with small groups working together with an adult.

In a family home, an excessive focus on keeping the children completely out of the kitchen can create its own risks. Young children may get themselves into trouble or simply create havoc if they are left in another room behind a shut door or gate. They are safer with their childminder, nanny or parent in the kitchen, but sitting in a safe location within the room. Children can sit safely at the kitchen table or low breakfast bar. Younger children will need a suitable seat. Children often like to be doing something related to the adult's domestic activity. If that is not possible, then table-top activities like drawing or play dough will keep hands busy and leave scope for conversation. The narrow galley kitchens in a few homes can be especially awkward, because there is very little room. Perhaps children could be seated safely at a little table or on the floor just outside.

Safe behaviour with crockery

Very young children need unbreakable cups and plates. But three- to five-year-olds are ready to learn care with proper crockery and glasses which, after all, form part of the equipment of a normal home.

When I visited Grandpont Nursery School they had a museum corner where the display included china jugs. Earlier in the year the home corner ran as a pretend café and was equipped with proper crockery. The practitioners took time to talk with the children about the difference between plastic and china, which the children could see and feel. They all talked about being careful because china can break. There were no breakages while the café was running and the museum corner has remained safe and intact.

Gardening

Children can enjoy the opportunities of gardening, and can learn about growth while gaining knowledge of the appropriate use of tools. As with other practical activities, real tools work best: plastic rather than metal gardening tools often bend or even snap as children try to work the earth. Good quality suppliers provide proper tools, adjusted where necessary for smaller hands and bodies (see, for instance, www.earlyexcellence.com/resource_outdoor_play.html or www.mindstretchers.co.uk). In gardening, as with other practical activities, practitioners should talk with children, as well as show them, how to use gardening tools effectively and in safety.

Safe behaviour with gardening tools

When I visited Windale First School, some of the reception class children were involved in gardening. One group was digging in potatoes and onions in the bed outside and another was potting seedlings in bought compost inside. Both of these activities were led by a parent who had chosen to spend the morning in the class.

At group time before lunch, the nursery teacher took time to review some of the morning's activities. The gardening group was encouraged to talk about the tools they had used and to reflect in words with their peers on 'How do we carry our spade?' and to demonstrate to their peers 'How do we carry our fork?' The teacher confirmed their explanation with: 'Yes we hold it down like this.' She then asked, 'Do we run?' and the group called out: 'No, we walk.'

The children at Grandpont Nursery are also enabled to use proper tools when they work in their garden. Careful behaviour is again coached through conversation and demonstration. The discussion about use of garden rakes covers points like: 'We hold the rake like this. We never wave it around.' The practical guidance of 'We never let the rake come up higher than our waist' has also made sense when generalised to how the children handle their hockey sticks for a game.

The nursery teacher described how this active involvement of the children helps them understand the consequences of their behaviour in a very positive way, that what they do has an impact on other people. Children cannot gain this understanding, nor confidence in tool use, if they spend all their time passively watching an adult using a tool. Children need the active first hand experiences.

Involvement of children in gardening raises issues around hygiene and keeping safe. Everyone needs to wash their hands after a gardening session and before any break to have a snack or picnic lunch outdoors. Depending on the situation, part of regular safety actions by practitioners can involve checking the outdoor space before children go outside on any day. In some neighbourhoods a range of unsafe objects are thrown into the gardens of nurseries and schools.

Some settings experience problems with local dog owners who allow their animals to use accessible front yards or grounds as a dog toilet. One London nursery was shocked to realise that some local people actually lifted their dog over the wall to let it mess in the nursery garden before being assisted back onto the pavement. It is appropriate that the staff clear up the results but explain to children what they are doing. It is certainly worth considering the example of some settings who made notices with the children to provoke some sense of shame in irresponsible grown-ups. If a courteous request makes minimal difference, a possibility is to send photos of any kind of messy vandalism to the local newspaper.

Construction, simple DIY and crafts

Three-, four- and five-year-olds are ready to learn practical crafts as well as have some involvement in simple mending activities that are part of the domestic routine of home or nursery. Real tools are safer in the long run and adult energy needs to be directed towards coaching children in a responsible approach to tools as well as some handy techniques. A wide range of arts, crafts, woodwork and simple needlework that works with blunt-ended needles is possible with older under-fives and children in the early years of primary school and out-of-school provision.

Children can gain in confidence and satisfaction in both the process and the end product when they reach this stage. They benefit from a well-organised learning environment where they know where to find tools and learn the importance of replacing them in a safe way. Children will be able to locate what they want with the help of written labels supported by pictures. Many settings use tool boards with the outline shape of the tool which fits onto the particular hook.

Adults are important at the coaching stage whenever children join the group, whether from the base room for younger children or those joining the setting for the first time. Adults can be important in reassuring children less experienced than their peers, or older children who took time to learn the skills and techniques they now use with confidence. The coaching process has to start anew with each child as does the useful reminder to look carefully and 'watch what your hands are doing'.

Individual practitioners and teams have to reach considered decisions about the level of independence offered to children and apply that decision in a consistent manner. Once children understand how to behave with sewing materials or at the woodwork table, they probably will not need any closer supervision than for any other activity. If the children have learning or physical disabilities, the level of supervision needs to be adjusted according to individual needs. However, different places have different ground rules: some settings decide that there is always an adult by the woodwork table and other senior teams have judged that children with experience of how to behave safely can access the same kind of facility without continuous adult supervision.

Whatever the project, it is important that children are enabled to take their time. A construction project or chosen craft activity may last all day, sometimes all week. Children appreciate a workshop atmosphere where there is somewhere to keep their work in progress safe while they take a break during the day or return to it the next day. There should be no pressure to complete everything in one session, although some work may have a naturally short time span.

Safe use of construction tools

Grandpont Nursery School regularly finds that parents are most uneasy about the prospect of the real woodwork table that includes proper-sized hammers, pliers, a hand drill, saws, nails and sandpaper. The staff explain how they help children to learn and they answer any questions from parents on their first visit and at the tea party for families new to Grandpont.

When children join the nursery they are shown carefully how to use the tools; handy techniques are shared, such as holding a nail with pliers and then hammering it into the wood. Children are welcome to start with soft wood before progressing to wood of normal hardness. No child at the woodwork table has ever had more than an ordinary scrape or very minor graze.

The end of morning group time at Windale reception class included a chance for the sewing group to speak up in a similar way to the children who had been gardening (p. 57). Young children answered the question, 'When we're doing our sewing, what do we have to do?' with confident replies of, 'Sit down; don't move about' and 'Watch our needle very carefully'. In Windale, the larger and sharper scissors are just for adults and the children were well able to answer the question, 'Who uses the special scissors?' with, 'The big people' and 'An adult'.

During their Forest School sessions, the children from Bridgwater Children's Centre are shown how to use knives, saws and tenon saws. They learn these skills over the months of their year of visits, understanding the best techniques and following the few safety rules. For instance, only adults carry the tenon saws across the woodland spaces.

8 Travelling Around

Young children will always be with a responsible adult, but the time will come when they need reliable skills for independent travel. It is all too easy for adults to let the years, and the opportunities for learning, pass by. Then young adolescents find themselves anxious because they lack any useful experience of how to plan a journey, keep track of landmarks, what to do if something goes wrong in the travel arrangements or if they get lost. It is very useful to have a mobile phone for calling home and for emergencies. But it is preferable that older children and young adolescents are not regularly calling for a pick-up because they are unable to use public transport when it is available.

Benefits as well as risk assessment

It is expected that practitioners undertake a risk assessment related to trips out from any setting. The official stance from government seems to be moving in a more sensible direction, to counteract messages, or fearful interpretations, that piles of paperwork are required before anyone steps out of the front door.

Repetitive risk assessment over very ordinary activities has not all been generated by over-anxious practitioners. For instance, the wording of the first edition of the Welfare Requirements of the English Early Years Foundation Stage in 2007 gave the strong impression that settings had to do a new risk assessment every time they went to the park. The revised edition (DCSF, 2008) gave the more sensible direction that risk assessments had to exist on each type of outing and should be looked at each time before people set out on that specific kind of trip.

There are significant benefits of getting young children out and about. Hopefully, the families of many children will recognise the value of what can seem to adults like mundane events. However, children are ready to find great interest in a visit to the post office or browsing in the market, which adults have experienced many times. Given these experiences, children find pleasure in outings that do not require a family entrance ticket. Apart from the intrinsic interest of the local neighbourhood, children start to learn about how to travel safely because they spend time accompanied by adults who help them to understand.

Practitioners working in sessional provision may have less scope for getting out and about. But it is possible to hear about and make suggestions for local possibilities through partnership with families. Early years practitioners who work in full day provision need to get out with children into the local area. In urban or more rural areas there is always somewhere to go. Babies and very young toddlers will need to be in buggies, ideally the type that face the adult, so it is easy to engage them in conversation. As soon as children are confident walkers, they need plenty of experience of using their legs. Some children have very limited experience of walking within their local neighbourhood because they spend their time travelling by car.

Children lose opportunities for learning when every trip is planned, run and navigated by adults. So plan child-focused outings.

- Think about what will engage individual children and small groups, on the basis of their current interests and what they talk about.
- Find out about what the children might like to revisit. Notice their interest at the time and invite them to say so as soon as they can express preferences in words.
- Be ready to stop and stare with children along the route; avoid thinking, 'But the point is to get to the library,' when the walk there is so full of interest.
- Make sure that any outing has enough time, so that children can really take part in the trip. Local outings driven by adults' pace and interests tend to reduce children to passive onlookers.

Planning and navigating

When planning a local trip, it is possible to share some of the organisation with the children.

- Talk together in advance about the route to the local market and envisage together what there may be to do and see. This conversation may be quite short with younger children, but they will then feel part of the forthcoming trip.
- Four- and five-year-olds are ready for a short conversation along the lines of 'how shall we get there?' Children of this age have a limited ability to imagine even familiar journeys, but they will learn with practice.
- The children can make the decision between alternative routes for the outward and the return journey. The decision might be to go out 'past the big building with the blue sign' and come back 'past Sasha's house because then we can go into the little park'.
- During the trip, talk about which local landmarks will soon be in view. It may be the postbox 'where we post the nursery letters', the big tree 'where we sometimes see that black cat' or the baker's 'where we buy those nice rolls'. Young children enjoy the anticipation of 'soon we'll see…'.
- Help children to focus on their surroundings by stopping at a corner or other decision point along the route and asking, 'Which way do we go now?' Give the children time to see if they can work it out.
- Young children will not yet understand the concepts of right and left, so support the words with gestures that show as well as tell. For example, 'We turn left at the traffic lights and left is this way', using arm gestures as appropriate.
- Perhaps each local trip will have one or two 'child navigators' who guide the group, with discreet help, when necessary, from the adult.
- Over time, the children will join up their local 'mental maps' and familiar adults help this process with comments such as, 'Oh look, we've come out by the…' or, 'Here we are, we walked to the market a different way today.'

Using public transport

Young children enjoy the first hand experience of going on a bus, train or tram. This opportunity may seem easier to offer in family life, with parents, nanny or childminder. However, some nurseries do organise regular outings for small groups of children to travel with their key person on the bus into the local town centre. Familiar adults can show children how this kind of travel works.

- Explain about buying a ticket, or using a pre-loaded card (a bit of a mystery to children at the outset) for adults or older children. Young children will probably travel free on some transport, but explain that this concession does not continue forever.

■ Without getting into too much detail, share any checking of the timetable or the map showing relevant stops. Children are often interested in how many more stations or bus stops there are to go, 'before it's our turn to get off' and like to count on their fingers.

■ Take every opportunity to spot familiar places or walking routes from the bus or train, perhaps seeing well-known landmarks from a very different angle. For example: 'Look, it's the common. It really is. It just looks different from the train.'

■ Sometimes the journey itself is the trip, especially useful if there is a circular route. There does not always have to be an end point where everyone gets off and does something else before the return journey.

Finding each other

When out in the street, younger children should always be close to the familiar adult – either in the buggy or holding a hand. Depending on the situation, three- to five-year-olds should be very close by, if not necessarily always holding the hand of an adult or another child. In safe and contained settings, children can begin to learn about being a short distance away, up to an agreed boundary.

For instance, one or more practitioners could take a group to visit the local library, spend time in the children's section and select a bag of books to borrow. Children will need to spread out to look at and choose their books.

■ Explain to them that the whole group stays within this area – adults as well as children. Look for a visual marker and say, for example, that nobody goes beyond 'this door' or 'this display'.

■ Adults can move about giving assistance where needed and ensure that children can see and wave to them. Keep them in sight.

On a local trip with two or more adults, it is possible to divide into small groups and plan to meet up later.

■ Make clear arrangements between the adults, but in such a way that children can hear, be part of the plan and recognise an easy meeting landmark.

■ The individual adults can encourage children's active memory by asking before everyone meets up again: 'So, who remembers where we have to meet Sophie and Jon?' Adults can also ask who wants to be the 'navigator' to guide the small group back to the meeting place.

- Older children of primary school age can be allowed to move around within a contained area, such as a museum display, small art gallery or enclosed city farm.
- Talk through where and when everyone will meet while everyone is standing close by the meeting place. Point out and involve the children in identifying useful landmarks to this location. Make sure somebody in each small group or pair has a watch and can tell the time.
- The adults responsible for the group need to reassure the children that they will never leave the given area without everyone. Adult safe behaviour of head counting at significant points shows children that they mean what they have promised.
- Sometimes it also helps to point out the main desk and the uniformed staff of a museum or gallery. Explain to children that large buildings often have a tannoy system to bring together people who have temporarily lost each other.

Road safety

Road safety skills are learned over the years of childhood and into early adolescence. Parents have a continuing responsibility to help their own children learn how to be safe around roads and traffic. At different points over the span of childhood, familiar practitioners will make an important contribution to this learning – in early years, school and out-of-school provision. However, it is important to challenge, in a friendly way, any parents who suggest that the full responsibility for coaching children in road safety rests with their nursery, school or out-of-school club. Partnership will be supported through different forms of communication. Conversation, display books or material on a provision's website help disseminate age-appropriate ideas on how to help. The same channels of communication can explain the contribution made by experiences organised for children or the value of regular routines, such as the walk to club led by practitioners who pick up from local primary schools.

Child pedestrians

Practitioners or parents need to understand the perspective of young children. It is equally important to realise that the most effective approach is first hand experience of real practice by the kerb side, with a familiar adult to ensure that children do not suffer from the consequences of misjudgements about safety.

Useful road safety research projects have highlighted how children actually think and behave, rather than how adults assume they operate. Road safety drills and codes sometimes start with rules and principles for children which they are then expected to apply to the actual situation. In fact, children younger than eight or nine years of age most often operate the other way around. They learn as the result of specific experiences, from which they are then able, with adult support, to work out more general rules to apply in the future.

To help children learn about road safety, it is crucial to look through their eyes – for an understanding of what they know of the world and also to look at things literally from their height.

- Young children have difficulty in judging both speed and distance with the accuracy that is required to assess whether it is, or is not, safe to cross before that vehicle approaching from the distance.
- Traffic codes for children have often stressed that they should 'find a safe place to cross'. But younger children do not understand the features that make a location safe or dangerous. They overlook the fact that they can be 'invisible' to drivers or cyclists, most dangerously if the child emerges from between two parked cars.
- Children sometimes judge wrongly that the shortest route between two points must be the safest, or that safety is increased by running. Child logic is that these choices reduce the time actually spent on the road.

Practitioners, and parents, need to utilise the opportunities that are a natural part of local outings to learn about road safety. Responsible adults always follow the safety rules when accompanied by children, even if time is running short.

- Say words out loud to make explicit how to behave safely. Familiar adults bear the full responsibility of keeping young children safe. But even two- and three-year-olds learn from an adult explanation such as, 'We're waiting because I can see those cars coming. Look over there' or, 'I can hear a bus coming round that corner. Listen, can you hear it?'
- Use a proper crossing whenever possible and alert children to the meaning of the 'green person' and the 'red person'.
- When there is no crossing, show children how to find a place where it is possible to see what is coming. Four- and five-year-olds will be ready to take part in a short discussion about, 'Is this a safe place to cross?'

- Use simple rules such as Stop–Look–Listen, and keep listening and looking. Younger children will not understand 'look right and left', so focus on looking 'both ways' or 'this way and then this way'.
- Establish the safe habit of stopping talking when crossing the road, in order to focus on listening and looking.

First hand experience – guided practice in real-life situations – is key to children's learning about road safety. Stories, puppets or road-safety rhymes may strengthen learning, as can talking about safety as it arises in the children's play with cars or roadways. However, these activities can only support; they will not substitute for real practice.

Children on wheels

Children need to learn safe behaviour when riding any bicycle or a scooter. Sound advice is to wear the right-sized helmet, done up properly, when cycling on pavements or cycle paths. Any adult cycling alongside a child should set a good example by wearing a helmet. It is a considered judgement about when children should transfer to cycling on the road. The Child Accident Prevention Trust suggests around 11 years of age (www.capt.org.uk/safety-advice/keeping-your-child-safe-bike) but it will be parents who make that final decision, considering the nature of the local roads.

Practitioners within group provision are most likely to deal with children and wheeled vehicles within the boundaries of the setting's outdoor spaces. There are plenty of valuable opportunities within that context for helping children develop habits of safe riding, for themselves and other people. Responsible teams work out, in consultation with the children, where the riding takes place and problem-solve any situations when enthusiastic bikers ride close to children busy with other enterprises. Under-fives can become adept in riding – sometimes even on two wheels – and they need experiences that teach them how to change direction and stop.

Parents, nannies and possibly childminders are more likely to need to address safety issues around children riding bikes and scooters on the pavement. The wide range of bikes and three-wheeled scooters means that under-fives can easily be in charge of a wheeled vehicle.

- Familiar adults need to be sure that young children can fully control the bike or scooter. They need to be able to change direction safely and stop easily before they are riding on the pavement.

- A sudden loss of control can mean, at best, that children collide with a person or a parked car. The worst case scenario is that they veer onto the road itself and into the path of a vehicle which is unable to stop.
- It is also wise to have firm ground rules about how far ahead a child can cycle or scoot and definitely stopping at the kerb of any road, however minor, that has to be crossed. This last rule also applies to walking children who can be trusted to go a little ahead.

Balanced decisions about safety headgear

There is good reason to establish a safety habit with children that they wear an appropriate helmet when they cycle – initially accompanied by an adult – in public areas like pavements, cycle or tow paths. The team of the Rainbow Centre (Marham) had to consider whether this advice should apply to an enclosed private outdoor area.

The team was given firm advice from a local road safety officer that children should wear helmets for riding any wheeled vehicle in their garden. The negative consequence of following this directive was that many children stopped using the bikes and scooters. Road safety matters but, during my consultancy with Rainbow, I agreed that insisting on helmets was a protective step too far.

Young children were losing the benefits of one source of physically active play, about which they were enthusiastic. There had been no biking accidents within the centre and children were capable of learning – from their own parents – that everyone should wear a helmet when biking outside the centre or family garden.

The argument that children might have an accident while riding the bikes applied potentially to any kind of lively physical activity. Given that

logic, children in Rainbow would have been wearing helmets for a considerable amount of their spontaneous, adventurous play in the garden, as one can see from the images of the outdoors at The Rainbow Centre on their website www.raf.mod.uk/rafmarham/stationfacilities/rainbow.cfm

The Rainbow team, like any group of practitioners, made their professional judgement about a less-than-certain health and safety issue and were able to communicate the rationale to the parents. The decision was to stop insisting that children put on helmets in the enclosed garden area. There have been no biking accidents in the two-and-a-half years since my consultancy with Rainbow.

The point of this example is not to disrespect advice from other professionals. The Rainbow team had followed the advice of the professionals but then realised that they needed to consider the bigger risk–benefit picture. Early years, school and out-of-school practitioners need to be able to make these assessments and communicate in a professional way the 'what' and 'why' of a decision taken. The communication may be in conversation, for instance with parents, but also in the written format of a risk–benefit assessment when appropriate.

Security and self-protection

There are three main strands to dealing with personal safety:

1. a safe balance in any provision between welcome access to parents and others who have legitimate reasons to visit, and security against intruders
2. sufficient security so that children cannot wander off without anybody realising
3. age-appropriate ways for children to learn steadily about personal safety.

Nurseries and schools need sensible measures that protect without turning the building and grounds into a fortress. Some provision is located in genuinely less safe neighbourhoods. Families who live in unsafe neighbourhoods are only too aware of the real hazards from which they are trying to protect their children and adolescents. But it is counter-productive when settings create the false impression of danger, when this is not the case for the majority of parents or children. Settings need to take steps proportionate to a realistic assessment of the need for security.

- It is appropriate to be able to monitor who is at the door and who comes in and out of a setting. It is not safe for people to simply wander in, or for children to wander out, without somebody being immediately aware of it.
- CCTV is now very common but is not necessarily a viable option for every setting. Furthermore, technology does not alone do the security job without further adult energy and alertness. Even the best system relies on sensible and consistent behaviour by adults.
- The low-technology option that is crucial for all settings still involves taking effective steps to shut front doors, or intervening doors in some buildings, and having a reliable system to lock front or garden gates to keep children safely inside. All staff, parents and legitimate visitors share this important responsibility.
- Managers or nursery owners have to make well-informed judgements about the area: about the genuine risks of daytime intruders and overnight break-ins or vandalism. Burglar alarms systems are very common, including in many family homes. Explain to children, if they ask, about highly visible measures like grilles on the windows.

Learning about personal safety

During early childhood responsible adults do most of the job of keeping young children safe. But the learning journey towards being able to keep themselves as safe as possible begins in these early years.

- Children need to learn steadily how to keep themselves safe without believing that it is entirely their responsibility. Adults – familiar and unknown – are responsible for behaving properly and not putting children in an uncomfortable or difficult position. Adults should behave within the rules of fair and considerate behaviour.
- Children should not be put at risk by otherwise well-meaning adults who impose blanket rules such as, 'You must be polite to adults' or 'Don't shout'. The behaviour of some adults means they no longer deserve politeness and some situations require shouting or yelling as a means to keeping safe.
- Ways of approaching personal safety with children should not focus exclusively on 'stranger danger'. Children are not helped by an unrealistic view of the world that generates anxiety about dangers lurking behind every bush. Another risk in focusing only on 'strangers' is that children soon regard an unknown or scarcely known person as safe, so long as they are pleasant. Additionally, children are mostly ill-treated or abused by people they know (Lindon, 2008).

A constructive approach to coaching children in personal safety includes children's rights over their own bodies and imparting the knowledge that there are private areas to one's body. Children need to be encouraged to speak about anything that concerns them, and should, of course, be reassured by a sympathetic and listening adult. The focus on telling can be linked with the idea that nobody has to keep a secret that makes them unhappy or uncomfortable. Exploration of this area of safety with children should be done in partnership with parents and as part of a process that will stretch into older childhood (Lindon, 2008).

Another theme is for adults to be honest when they enforce safety measures with the group. Children notice and are less anxious or frightened if their familiar adult explains, rather than dismisses their concern with a 'never mind'. For instance, you might say, 'I brought us out of the post office, because that woman was getting very angry and was swearing. We'll go back later when she's gone'; or, 'Yes, I think that man was very drunk and he was getting silly and rude. We don't need that.'

Be prepared to talk with children about an uncomfortable or unpleasant incident if they so desire. They may also wish to play it out. In the kind of event implied above, it would make sense, for example, to mention it to the parents when they come to pick up children at the end of the day. Children are likely to mention out of the ordinary events and it is preferable that parents hear the details from a fellow adult. They will feel reassured that their child's key person or childminder handled the situation in a responsible way.

A safe enough environment for free movement

Like other settings with a strong commitment to the outdoors, the team of the Rainbow Centre (Marham) have created an outdoors environment in which children can roam about freely and where they will sometimes be out of sight. The physical boundaries are secure and careful attention is paid to the maintenance of equipment and the grounds. Babies and toddlers stay in sight but, once they are mobile, toddlers can stretch the invisible elastic by choosing to go further in their dedicated outdoor space.

The over-threes have considerable choice of movement outdoors and the centre runs a free-flow system for much of the day. Practitioners are spread through the garden, as well as indoors, but they trust the children to use the more secluded outdoor areas, like the willow structure. During my visit I could see how these still-young children were enthusiastic about using the resources yet were able to call on an adult easily. They also understand, as one child explained to me, that in the last part of the afternoon, they do not go round the corner to another part of the garden. The out-of-school club uses that space over that period.

9 Partnership with Parents

In every kind of daily provision, practitioners share the responsibility and duty of care with the children's family. Parents have a continuing responsibility towards their sons and daughters stretching into later childhood and young adulthood. Practitioners should never imply that they are taking over that obligation for the duration that children attend a nursery or a childminder's home. However long and positive the relationship, children and their families will eventually move on. Partnership with families matters a great deal and has different strands (Lindon, 2009a) starting from the earliest contacts.

Early contact with parents

First conversations with parents, or other family carers, need to establish the atmosphere of a dialogue between the family and the setting. This tone is as relevant for safety issues as for any other aspects of practice. The first step is to make parents feel welcome to visit the setting before their child starts and offer an atmosphere in which it is easy to ask questions or make comments. Many settings offer the option of one or two practitioners visiting the family home. Parents can express a preference not to have this home visit, but many welcome the chance to have an initial chat in their familiar space.

Whether an individual childminder or a team member of a group provision, the need is to communicate a consistent message and a responsible approach to safety. The details should reassure parents that practitioners will take very good care of babies, toddlers and children.

■ Avoid giving long lists of hazards of which the team is aware. There is then a risk of giving parents the impression that a nursery or childminder's home is a dangerous place.

■ Communicate the aim to create an environment in which children can learn to manage risks appropriate to their developmental understanding.

■ Consider ways to get across the professional commitment that a safe enough environment is one in which children are able to take manageable risks and to assess their own risk – appropriate to their age.

■ At an early stage of partnership with families, it is wise to get across that an enjoyable and playful childhood will include some bumps, scrapes and bruises. But also explain the care taken to prevent the avoidable accidents and deal with the unavoidable.

■ The general message – of enjoyable play and first hand experiences – needs to be supported by spoken or visual examples: photos, showing parents around provision during a working day or materials on the website.

■ An early conversation, revisited as necessary, needs to make clear to parents that children will go outdoors a great deal and why this is so important.

■ Extra care will be taken for children with fragile health. Otherwise it is unwise for practitioners to go along with parents who require high standards of 'good enough weather' for their child to go outdoors.

■ Active play will mean that sometimes children or their clothes are far from pristine at the end of a day or session. Ideally children come equipped with their own outdoor clothing but settings often gather sunhats, wellington boots or other useful top layer clothing for the weather.

■ The health and safety policy should be easily available for parents to read, just like any of the other policies and procedures.

■ Be ready to follow up any concerns through individual conversations, which explain to parents what is done, how and why, rather than offering blanket 'Don't worry' reassurances or the get-out clause of, 'We have to. It's health and safety.'

Everything of significance will not be said in one long conversation. Continued partnership means that practitioners revisit, in ways personal to the toddler or child, the learning journey of the child towards sharing in their own care and growing skills of self-reliance. Continued communication with parents reassures them that their child's key person or childminder is ready to listen and takes a genuinely individual approach. Some parents may wish to discuss what they see as their child's over-confidence, leading him or her into excessive risk-taking. Other parents may be looking for a supportive boost for their child whom they see as overly anxious, or still recovering from an accident that has shaken confidence.

Parents of disabled children want practitioners to address the individual needs of their child and not a general disability label. Some parents may behave in ways that get them labelled as 'over-protective' of disabled sons and daughters. Sensitive practitioners work to understand and respect the source of such feelings. However, parents may be keen that their child's spontaneous play is not restricted unduly and only too pleased that their child's key person or childminder envisages the odd bruise or the grubbiness that comes with ordinary play.

Meeting parents' concerns with respect

Parents are not reassured by blanket reassurances such as, 'we're all professionals here. Of course your children will be fine.' Parents reasonably want practitioners to listen to any reservations they feel about equipment within the permanent play provision for children or any unease about a proposed outing.

The settings named and described in this book all took care to anticipate likely questions or concerns. Practitioners were willing and pleased to deal in a personal way with any reservations. The team of Grandpont Nursery were ready to talk through wariness from some families about the woodwork table. The approach of Bridgwater Forest School reflects the strand in the Forest School movement of establishing clear channels of communication with parents. Skerne Park reception class had taken the approach common to many outdoors projects and had organised a special family session in the woodland. Most parents had joined their children and photos from that event were part of wall displays in reception class and children's personal folders.

Continued communication in partnership

Good overall practice is to keep the channels of communication open with parents. Sometimes this communication will be about safety, risk taking and encouragement for the child to be more independent in an age-appropriate way. Conversations with individual parents may include, for example, what Kenny managed today in terms of balancing along the planks set on the milk crates. In return parents should feel comfortable to share with their child's key person or childminder that at home Kenny is keen to help with the new baby, but they are uneasy about whether it is safe to let him.

Partnership with parents means taking opportunities to talk through current shared enterprises with children as well as their self-chosen projects, some of which will be undertaken with friends. Conversations with parents may also help some of them to appreciate more fully the process of their child's work and not just the impact of that day's end-product. For instance, a child may have spent a considerable amount of the session hand-drilling holes in a piece of wood or redoing a piece of needlework to their own satisfaction. Apart from the efforts of the day, the child may return to the project as a work in progress.

Perhaps children, as another example, have greeted the prospect of making their own magazine with great enthusiasm. There will be opportunities to use more grown-up stationery tools like a stapler or hole puncher. Practitioners can share the flexible plans with parents, including the aim that children will learn how to use these tools in a safe way. Reassure uneasy parents that it is much safer in the long run to show younger children how to use a tool properly than leave them to find an unsafe way of using them as an unsupervised older child. It is safer to provide children with a single hole puncher and show them how to use it, than have children use their initiative, without the safety knowledge, and try to make holes by forcing through the points of scissors.

In reality, many parents are not uneasy about their children being taught practical skills and may be swift to extend what they do at home from ideas that clearly work in nursery, primary school or out-of-school club. Uneasy practitioners sometimes cite pressure from parents as the reason for their own very cautious approach. Yet Forest School and other woodland projects are usually popular with families. Informal conversations with parents, which helped to shape the content of this book, were far more often about their frustrations at over-cautious practice or the non-discussion of bans of games that children enjoyed.

Sharing ideas with families may include the display of what is sometimes called 'warm technology': hand-held and controlled. A hand drill is far simpler to control than a major power tool. Children cannot be left alone to work a food processor or electric beater, although they will benefit from watching a clear example from an adult of how to be safe. Yet keen young cooks can use a simple hand whisk and learn to operate a hand beater. Children may pass on tips to their parents, for instance that it is better to have separate pairs of scissors for cutting paper and for fabric. Cutting paper blunts the edges of scissors and the same pair will soon make a mess of cutting fabric.

Parents will usually sign a general agreement form about regular local trips that are organised with the children, by group settings or childminders. Special trips need an additional specific agreement, covering details about the outing: what, when and where. A covering letter would explain what children would need, including clothing and any costs involved. Without over-elaborating, the letter might be an opportunity to describe how any safety aspects will be handled or hygiene issues tackled, for instance during a farm visit. Parents will be welcome to ask further questions of their child's key person or the named practitioner who has taken on the main responsibility for this special trip.

When there has been an incident

Most parents are reasonable and it is crucial that no practitioner develops, unchallenged, a negative view of the parent group as a whole based on a few argumentative or highly anxious individuals. However, the most fair-minded parents will become uncooperative if they are treated with disrespect. A sense of false partnership arises when practitioners are careless about ensuring communication after an incident, or when parents' practical questions about a trip are dismissed as fussing or a challenge. The few parents who were critical of safety issues or standards, within informal conversations related to this book, were irritated for these very reasons.

More general communication with parents can be appropriate when something has happened outside the setting which nevertheless affects many or all of the children. A setting may have to face the fact, for example, that a known child has been seriously injured or killed in an accident. After swift but considered thought, it may feel appropriate to send a letter to all families explaining the situation and the readiness in the setting to listen to children's feelings and concerns.

Increased willingness to sue?

There is a level of anxiety that UK society is now very litigious and that parents are likely to sue a nursery or school at the slightest excuse. It is hard to get clear information but some commentators (Gill, 2007) point out that cases that reach court are not simply nodded through by compliant judges. Case law has established the responsibility of parents for their own younger children and that older children and young people share some of that responsibility in choices they make over their own risky behaviour. The general atmosphere also seems to have moved to a recognition that responsible adults have sometimes taken every appropriate action for safety. The rather irritating official mantra of 'lessons must be learned' implies that there will always be faults to be rectified. Yet accidents do happen; nobody is to blame and there are often no sensible changes left to be made in normal practice for health and safety.

The Young Report (2010) acknowledged anxieties about what has been called the 'compensation culture': a readiness to assign blame and seek financial recompense. The recommendations aim to address the consequences of invitations by some companies that there is money to be made by launching personal injury claims for just about any accident. However, there is an equal aim to ensure families are able to pursue incidents of failure in the duty of care or challenge failings in responsible health and safety. Of course, local authorities and the inspectorate need to be assiduous in following up questionable safety practice in any provision for children.

Even if myths or the reality of a compensation culture are more effectively addressed, the risk of an incident occurring cannot be reduced to zero. Practitioners and teams need to ensure that they have sound practice in place and can explain what they do and why. If parents are dissatisfied with a full explanation and threaten legal action, it is crucial to contact relevant people within the hierarchy of a nursery chain, management committee or local authority. A further step may need to be a representative from the legal department. Take their advice on how to proceed, including the nature of any further conversations with the parents.

Sometimes the legal representative of an organisation, local authority or the insurance company will decide that it is better to settle out of court than to fight a case. This decision can be made despite full confidence in the individual practitioner, team and their health and safety practice. Such a step can seem unjust and risks encouraging other families to try and gain financial compensation in the future. However, settling out of court is sometimes judged the safer option when the outcome of a full court case seems uncertain. People and organisations proven free of blame in a court case can nevertheless still be left with a substantial legal bill. Their costs are not necessarily met by the party who brought a case which has been judged to be groundless.

References and Further Resources

Ball, D. (2002) *Playgrounds – Risks, Benefits and Choices*, Health and Safety Executive, www.hse.gov.uk/research/crr_pdf/2002/crr02426.pdf

Ball, D., Gill, T. and Spiegal, B. (2008) *Managing Risk in Play Provision: Implementation Guide*, www.education.gov.uk/publications/

Cairns, W. (2008) *How to Live Dangerously: Why we Should All Stop Worrying and Start Living*, Macmillan.

Casey, T. (2010) *Inclusive Play: Practical Strategies for Children from Birth to Eight*, Sage.

Child Accident Prevention Trust (www.capt.org.uk). The leaflets *Getting Over An Accident* for parents and for professionals may go onto the website. But in 2011 a request has to be made by telephone on 020 7608 3828 or email at safe@capt.org.uk

Department for Children, Schools and Families (2008, second edition) *The Early Years Foundation Stage – Setting the Standards for Learning, Development and Care for Children from Birth to Five*, DCSF, www.teachernet.gov.uk/teachingandlearning/EYFS

Duckett, R. and Drummond, M.J. (2010) *Adventuring in Early Childhood Education*, Sightlines Initiative.

Free Play Network (2005) *Places for Play: Exhibition*. See also *Places of Woe, Places of Possibility* (exhibition), *No Risk. No Play?* (online discussion forum) and *Give us a Cuddle* (online discussion forum), www.freeplaynetwork.org.uk

Gill, T. (2007) *No Fear: Growing Up in a Risk-Averse Society*, Calouste Gulbenkian summary and full book on www.gulbenkian.org.uk

Gleave, J. (2008) *Risk and Play: a Literature Review*, Play England www.playday.org.uk/PDF/Risk-and-play-a-literature-review.pdf

Hawkins, C. (2010) 'Inflated view of risk inhibits children', *Nursery World* 11 November 2010.

Health and Safety Executive (www.hse.gov.uk/risk). The HSE offers a wide range of papers on risk and sensible risk management.

Inside-Out Nature (www.insideoutnature.co.uk). Source of the Danish outdoor cookware (Viking ware).

KIDS (www.kids.org.uk). KIDS works with disabled children, young people and their families. The organisation Kidsactive is now part of KIDS.

Kidscape (www.kidscape.org.uk). Kidscape focuses on safety, child protection and strategies to deal with bullying.

Lindon, J. (2006) *Helping Babies and Toddlers Learn: A Guide to Good Practice with Under-Threes*, National Children's Bureau.

Lindon, J. (2008) *Safeguarding Children and Young People: Child Protection 0–18 years*, Hodder Arnold.

Lindon, J. (2009a) *Guiding the Behaviour of Children and Young People: Linking Theory and Practice 0–18 years*, Hodder Arnold.

Lindon, J. (2009b) *Parents as Partners: Positive Relationships in the Early Years*, Practical Pre-School Books.

Lindon, J. (2010) *Child-Initiated Learning*, Practical Pre-School Books.

Lindon, J. (2011) *Planning for Effective Early Learning*, Practical Pre-School Books.

Madge, N. and Barker, J. (2007) *Risk and Childhood*, RSA, www.rsariskcommission.org.uk

Miller, J. (2003) *Never Too Young: How Young Children Can Take Responsibility and Make Decisions,* Save the Children.

Mindstretchers (2009) *Risk it*, www.mindstretchers.co.uk/articles/risk-it.html and other online articles on www.mindstretchers.co.uk/articles.html

NSPPC (2007) *Child abductions*, www.nspcc.org.uk/Inform/research/statistics/child_abductions_statistics_wda48733.html The NSPCC provides statistics and research papers about child protection at www.nspcc.org.uk/Inform/research/research_wda48228.html

O'Brien, L. and Murray, R. (2006) *A Marvellous Opportunity for Children to Learn: A Participatory Evaluation of Forest School in England and Wales*, Forestry Commission www.forestry.gov.uk/pdf/fr0112forestschoolsreport.pdf/$FILE/fr0112forestschoolsreport.pdf

Play Safety Forum (2002) *Managing Risk in Play Provision*, www.ncb.org.uk/Page.asp?origin x6168nj_19470950508125u96d3575202849

Rich, D. and others (2005) *First Hand Experience: What Matters to Children*, Rich Learning Opportunities.

Rogalski, H. (2010) *At What Age Can I? A Guide to Age Based Legislation*, Children's Legal Centre, www.childrenslegalcentre.com

Rowling, L. (2003) *Grief in School Communities: Effective Support Strategies*, Open University Press.

Royal Society for the Prevention of Accidents (www.rospa.com). The RoSPA focuses on advice and information about common risks and accident prevention.

Sightlines Initiative *The Rising Sun Woodland Pre-school Project*, DVD about adventurous outdoor learning, www.sightlines-initiative.com

Tovey, H. (2007) *Playing Outdoors: Spaces and Places, Risk and Challenge*, Open University Press.

Warden, C. (2007) *Nurture Through Nature*, Mindstretchers, www.mindstretchers.co.uk

Warden, C. (2010) *Nature Kindergartens*, Mindstretchers.

Williams-Siegfredsen, J. (2005) 'Run the risk', *Nursery World* 4 August 2005 www.insideoutnature.com/download/RunTheRiskArticle.pdf

Young Report (2010) *Common Sense, Common Safety* www.number10.gov.uk/wp-content/uploads/402906_CommonSense_acc.pdf

Index